11/80. 7.75

Reproducing Furniture in Miniature

Reproducing Furniture in Miniature

Ann Kimball Pipe

Contemporary Books, Inc.
Chicago

Published by Contemporary Books, Inc.
180 North Michigan Avenue, Chicago, Illinois 60601
Manufactured in the United States of America
Library of Congress Catalog Card Number: 79-51486
International Standard Book Number: 0-8092-8294-1 (cloth)
                                    0-8092-8072-8 (paper)

Published simultaneously in Canada by
Beaverbooks
953 Dillingham Road
Pickering, Ontario L1W 1Z7
Canada

Contents

Introduction

In the world of miniature make-believe there are two countries. The older one is for children only. It has traditionally been filled with wonderful things to play with, and among the most important of these are dollhouses. Historically, grown-ups have been permitted to build the houses and make enough small furniture to fill the rooms. Once the work was finished, however, an invisible "Keep Out" sign was promptly posted by the new owners, and the children, as they were meant to do, took over.

The other, newer country, the one for grown-ups only, is still not a new one. It is centuries old, but in recent years its population has been growing by leaps and bounds. Adults have found that making simple furnishings for the children's houses was such fun, they were tempted to go a step further. It was a challenge to work more detail into the pieces, to fill the woods, to upholster and carve and polish until, except for sizes, the reproductions could hardly be told from the original models.

When enough of these more refined and elegant pieces were done, they were sometimes placed on a shelf for display, arranged in miniature rooms with glass fronts or in a house which had been finished with the same attention to detail and proportion as had been given the furniture.

After such painstaking work, who would have the courage to turn these treasures over to the children to play with, to wear out, or break?

Because so many grown-ups kept their treasures, the second country was born. It is a place where children, very quietly and with permission, may come: They may look and admire and dream, but they may not touch. For this restriction they will be thankful in the years to come when they have children of their own and the lovely furniture is still intact. Then they will remember their own feelings when, years ago, they were allowed to stand and stare. Their own sons and daughters, in turn, will be taught to do the same until they too are grown and have children of their own.

It is for the grown-up youngsters of the second country that this book is written. Let the makers of toy furniture use it; they have our permission and are sure to find it very useful in their work. They should keep in mind, however, that at least for the time being, they are only guests in a land to which, sooner or later, they are almost certain to apply for full citizenship.

1

What To Make?

The purposes of this book are twofold—to explain, as clearly as possible, how to make miniature replicas of full-size furniture, and to demonstrate that the work is not nearly as difficult as the uninitiated may imagine. Anyone who has a talent for working with his hands, and who has the interest, can make small pieces of furniture which, if viewed in surroundings that are proportionally correct, could be mistaken for their full-size counterparts.

It has been said that it would be next to impossible to write simple instructions on how to put on a coat. Descriptions of the necessary gestures could so intimidate the unfortunate reader, he might decide it would be easier just to stay cold. This is true of almost anything new that is being learned; the doing is nearly always easier than the reading of how to do it.

There *are* ways, however, of getting that coat on a little faster. For example: Although the writer has been using small electric tools for many years, she had to learn a whole new vocabulary for this book. The "thingamajig" that had always slipped very easily into the "gizmo" of the lathe now became the "arbor chuck" that fit into the "headstock." Much of this new vocabulary, however, has been discarded in the following chapters. Although the headstock is no longer a gizmo, it will now be called the left end of the lathe, which is exactly what it is. Let the users of heavy, full-size power tools call it what they will.

The reader should also be told that although various forms of the word "perfect" have been used freely in this book, the writer is well aware that it is much easier to describe perfection than to produce it. No matter how carefully the measuring, sawing, and sanding have been done, imperfections are bound to appear when working with such small pieces. There will be occasions when a cut piece must be discarded, or plans must be changed. Two edges that seemed to fit exactly when held together may show a gap at one spot after they have been glued.

These small imperfections are to be expected and are annoying only if not corrected. That tiny gap will disappear if a dab of wood filler is smoothed into it. The drawer that shows a crack above it can, and should, be recut. The nick in the side panel where a tool slipped can be sanded away. While perfection should be the goal of the worker in miniatures, he should not be discouraged if he does not reach it in every piece he makes.

Similarly, because of the lack of more accurate words, "should" and "must" are used frequently in this book. There are times when it will be advisable for the reader to take them literally. More often, however, they should be translated as, "This is the method the writer uses," and the reader should ignore them if a new and better idea occurs to him. It is one of the many pleasures connected with the work that each new piece of furniture presents its own challenge to the craftsman's ingenuity, and if there were not always the possibility of finding a better way of doing anything, or of improving on the results, where would be the fun of doing it at all?

At the start, the craftsman who takes seriously the making of miniature replicas may as well face the fact that he will occasionally be introduced as the person who makes that "precious dollhouse furniture." Whatever he may say by way of explanation will leave the impression that he is anti-dollhouse, which he is not. It is far better, then, just to accept the introduction as a maker of toys than to attempt to explain the difference.

Actually, the important differences between miniature replicas and dollhouse furniture are only two: insofar as possible, all the details of the full-size model must be included in the small copy, and proportions must be exact.

Out-of-proportion pieces in a dollhouse have a certain charm. If the legs of a chair are too long, a bed too large or too small and a carpet too thick, the viewer is given the feeling of having stepped into a happy, imaginary world where nothing, not even size, is real. To see perfection in such a place would not even be particularly desirable.

If the maker of miniature replicas, however, keeps in mind the importance of precision as he works, the result will be not toys, but furniture close to works of art of which he will have reason to be proud.

Before starting his first piece, it would be wise for the reader to consider the general periods in history in which he would like to work. Even if his intention is to make only a few pieces for the sheer pleasure of the work involved, let him be warned that if others' experiences are a criterion, he will not stop there. He will probably make one more, then another and another until, without really having meant to, he will have accumulated enough furniture to fill at least one room.

Miniature furniture in styles of early twentieth century.

While it is not necessary that the furniture eventually be displayed in rooms or a miniature house, many craftsmen prefer to show it that way. Even if the plan at first is simply to display each piece as an end in itself, some thought given to periods and styles will enable the craftsman to group the pieces later into coordinated rooms. If the styles of those pieces cover a span of many hundreds of years, he may be hard-pressed to arrange them in a credible way.

This does not mean, however, that he should limit himself to a single period or even a single century. Unless he wishes to make only one style of furniture, such as Victorian or Chippendale, or to make an authentic record of a certain period in history, there is no reason why he cannot choose to combine several styles and periods covering two hundred years or so, just as he might when furnishing his own home.

Some makers of miniature furniture would not agree with the writer's feeling that, within limits, dates should remain flexible. They prefer to select a definite cutoff date, such as 1600 or 1700, and will make nothing belonging to a different period. This is a matter of personal preference, and each craftsman may plan any way he chooses as long as he does have a plan, or, at least, a general idea of what he would like to do.

Within reason, the historical time span the maker of miniature furniture allows himself is less important than the logic of the individual pieces he makes. For example: A person elects to work within the nineteenth and twentieth centuries. A dresser of the early nineteenth century is just as usable today as it was when new. Utilitarian pieces, such as radios, stoves, phonographs, and the like, are usually discarded when something that works better is invented. Therefore, while the antique dresser might very well live in harmony with a contemporary bed, a comparatively modern, battery-powered radio with a horn speaker would look incongruous in the same room.

If the craftsman wishes to put his furniture into miniature rooms or into a house, these should be made with the same care and attention to detail that he has given the furniture. It would be a mistake to put his beautiful pieces into a ready-made dollhouse with its flat, unmitered window frames and unpaneled doors. His rooms should have shaped floor and picture moldings, shaped edges on door panels, and floors that are covered with narrow boards instead of a single piece of wood. The stair treads should overhang the risers, and hand railings should not be simply flat strips of wood. Making such a house, or set of rooms will take time, but it is time well spent if rooms are to be used at all.

When a general period in which to work has been chosen, the next step is to select the first piece of furniture to be made. If there are to be any difficulties connected with making such a choice, it will not be from lack of sources of material. Library shelves are filled with furniture books, one's own home may be a source of favorite pieces, and homes of friends may offer more. Many art museums have a few rooms filled with priceless antique furniture, and permission to take pictures and measurements is usually given readily, once the purpose has been explained.

For those who share the writer's weakness for some of the low-priced, elaborate furniture that was mass-produced in the late nineteenth and early twentieth centuries, there are reprints to be found in bookstores of old Sears, Roebuck catalogs. In addition to furniture, these catalogs are a rich source of illustrations for such miscellaneous items as trunks, fern stands, sewing machines, musical instruments, coatracks and lamp shades—pictures that might be difficult to find elsewhere.

Trunk and guitar were copied from old Sears, Roebuck catalog. Kitchen match shows comparative sizes.

When selecting his first piece, the reader should keep in mind the tools that are available to him. This does not mean that if tools are limited, the piece must be kept simple. Very elaborate and beautiful miniatures can be made with just a jigsaw, some sandpaper, and glue.

A jigsaw is the only power tool needed to make all the pieces shown. This desk is 2 13/16 inches high.

A table intended for a dollhouse, for example, may consist of only five pieces—four legs and a top. These are sawed to shape, sanded and glued together. If the maker wishes to go a step further, he may cut four pieces for an apron and glue them into place. The table is now composed of nine pieces.

An elaborate Victorian table may consist of thirty or thirty-five pieces, but it is made in the same way as the dollhouse table. Each piece is sawed, sanded and glued into place. No additional skill or equipment is required; the only extra requirement is time.

One should not, however, choose to copy a spindle bed or a

Boston rocker unless he has a lathe. It is extremely difficult to carve identical spindles by hand. Likewise, only an experienced wood-carver should select a piece that requires carving unless he owns a hand drill with a speed that can be varied. With such a tool, and a little practice, even the inexperienced can learn to do excellent carving.

The time that might be required for making a certain piece should not influence the choice. It does not matter if, after a few

Victorian furniture, carved with hand drill.

weeks of leisure-time, pickup work, the craftsman has completed one piece, or four, or five. The trip along the way should be unhurried, and as important to his sense of accomplishment as the finished furniture itself will be.

2

Tools—Necessary and Optional

If the beginner does not yet own any tools with which to make miniature furniture, he will be happy to learn that an elaborate workshop is not only unnecessary, it is also next to impossible to have. Most of the standard power tools, even if they are needed for miniature work, are not available in sizes that can be used for very thin, small pieces of wood.

Every tool catalog carries enticing advertisements for special attachments that will do "small" work, but when one reads the fine print and the specifications, he realizes what a wide range the word "small" can cover. Very few of them can be used for the work covered in this book.

The jobs that some of the large tools do, moreover, are not necessary for working in miniature. A power router, for example, cuts grooves of various shapes which are used to make very strong joints in furniture. Not being able to make such joints is no handicap to the craftsman whose chairs will not be sat in day after day, nor whose dresser drawers will be pulled out and slammed shut hundreds of times a year. For permanent joints, such pieces require only a strong adhesive plus a few dowels where necessary.

Certain other power tools, such as a small shaper or a

planer, might simplify the craftsman's work, but are by no means necessities. Different ways can be found to do the same job, and finding these ways is part of the satisfaction of working in miniature.

Tools which the craftsman may wish to purchase are discussed in the following pages. Some of these tools are necessary, and some are optional. How to use these tools will be covered further along in the book.

Jigsaw

A jigsaw is the only power tool that is a must for making miniature replicas. It is such a versatile tool it can cut any piece desired from a large, straight-sided panel to a shaped rosette no more than $\frac{1}{8}$ inch across. No great skill is required in using it although, like anything else, the longer the craftsman does use it, the more expert he will become in making the more difficult cuts.

Compared to the prices of some of the larger power tools, a

A small jigsaw is needed for miniature work.

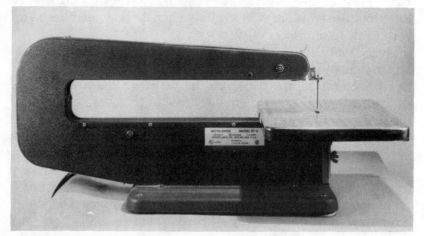

jigsaw of a size suitable for miniature work is not expensive. It would therefore be unwise for the craftsman to try to save a few dollars when selecting the one tool he will use more often in his work than any other.

The jigsaw he does select should have certain features. First, a good rotary motor is important. Some of the less expensive saws, such as those designed for use by children, have vibrating motors which do not allow the blade to cut smoothly.

Next, the jigsaw must have a table that can be tilted. This will enable the craftsman to cut beveled edges which are necessary when making mitered joints, or when joining the corners of flat pieces, such as those on picture frames.

The throat of the saw (the space between the blade and the back of the arm) should be as long as possible so that a piece of wood at least a foot long can be fed through the blade without its back edge being stopped by the arm.

The blade slot (the hole in the table through which the blade passes) should be as small as possible. The reason for this is explained fully in chapter 5, and while the craftsman will probably not have much choice in slot sizes, it is a point to remember in case he does.

A large, heavy jigsaw that is permanently mounted on a worktable and driven by a separate motor with a belt is neither needed nor desirable for cutting small pieces. The saw selected should be light enough to be carried easily and can be powered by an integral, very small horsepower motor.

Any jigsaw with the above features will be suitable for making miniature furniture. Such saws can usually be found in well-equipped hobby shops, in retail-store tool departments, and in the pages of mail-order tool catalogs.

If a choice of sizes is available for the saw selected, a few fine-toothed, medium-toothed, and wide blades should be purchased. The wide blade is especially helpful for making straight cuts. If there is no choice, however, the general-purpose blade made to fit the saw will be perfectly satisfactory for miniature work. A few extra blades should always be kept on hand; although they rarely break, they can do so if too great a strain is put on them. In any case, blades must be replaced occasionally, as they become dull.

Circular Saw

There are now on the market several brands of circular saws made specifically for miniature work. These saws can handle wood up to about ½-inch thick, and will make cuts whose edges are perfectly straight and true. If the saw selected has a blade that can be tilted to 45 degrees, it will also bevel edges. It cannot, however, saw curved lines or intricate shapes, and is therefore not a substitute for a jigsaw.

A small circular saw is useful for making straight cuts and beveling straight edges.

The blade of a circular saw is necessarily thicker than that of a jigsaw, and will therefore take a wider bite out of the wood as it cuts. This makes the tool more difficult to use for very fine work, but if there are to be two saws on the workbench, a circular saw will do special jobs quickly and easily, and will save the craftsman the trouble of straightening jigsaw-cut edges with a file.

Variable-Speed Drill

Second in importance to the craftsman will be a power hand

drill or "electric rotary grinder." There is probably a wider choice of such drills available than there are jigsaws. Some have set speeds, and some, speeds that can be varied. There are drills whose motors are in the handles of the tools, while others are attached to a separate motor by a flexible shaft. Some of these separate motors are operated by a foot pedal, others by a hand switch.

The hand drill the craftsman does select should have two

Electric-powered hand drill and pin vise.

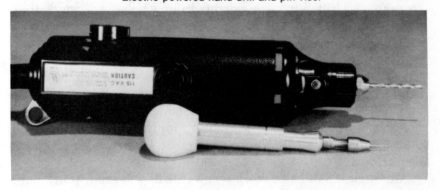

features: its speed should be variable, and it should be small enough to be handled easily in doing fine work. A variable speed is needed because the speed of a drill that cannot be changed is a high one, and slow speeds are often needed when precise, intricate work is being done.

Beyond these two points, the craftsman's choice will depend upon how much money he wishes to spend. A dental drill, found in dental supply houses, usually has a convenient small handle that holds the bit and can be used almost as easily as a pencil. It is connected to the motor by a flexible shaft and can be turned on and off by a foot pedal. However, such a drill is comparatively expensive.

The motor is contained in the handle of the type of variable-speed drill usually found in hobby shops, and while this makes the tool a little more unwieldy, it can still be handled easily enough to do any fine, detailed work necessary.

If the craftsman already owns a hand drill whose high speed cannot be varied, an attachment is available that will allow him to slow it down. Such an arrangement is a little less convenient to use than is a built-in control, but perfectly possible to use with good results.

Even if the selected power drill comes in a set which includes accessories, the set probably does not include an assortment of drill bits and carving bits (also called "burrs") suitable for very fine work. A few of these should therefore be purchased separately. Drill bits are used for drilling holes, and since the very thin ones do break occasionally, a few spares with diameters about equal to those of pins and thin brads should be included in the assortment selected.

Carving bits come in a variety of shapes—round, elliptical, cylindrical, vertical-cone, and so on. Although most hobby shops offer a selection of these very small, shaped bits, a wider selection can usually be found in dental supply houses. The craftsman should make sure that whatever he buys will fit his particular drill.

Although for full-size work a power drill will sand, rout, and shape edges, and grind, carve and drill holes, in miniature work the drill will be used mostly for carving and for drilling holes in both metal and wood. However, these two operations are so important to his work that if the craftsman does own a variable speed drill, he will find it to be one of his most-used tools.

Pin Vise

Although a pin vise is not a motor-operated tool, it should be mentioned here as an alternative to the electric drill.

A pin vise is a small tool, only a few inches long, that can do one thing only—it can hold drill bits for easy hand-drilling of holes in wood. It does that one thing so well, however, that even though one may also own an electric drill, he is apt to lay it aside on occasion and use the pin vise instead.

That occasion is usually when a small hole is to be placed so exactly it must not be even an unmeasurable distance off. Such a hole is needed, for example, when two pieces are to be joined by a dowel, and one hole must exactly meet the hole in the other piece of wood. While accurately placed holes can also be made with an electric drill, the fact that the pin vise turns only when the operator manipulates it by hand makes possible very slow and accurate work. Drilling a fairly large hole all the way through a thick piece of wood, however, would be difficult to do with a pin vise.

It is necessary that the craftsman have either a power drill or a pin vise, but since the latter costs only a dollar or two, the ideal arrangement is that he have both.

Lathe

A lathe is the last of the power tools the craftsman may wish to use. It is possible for him to furnish entire miniature rooms without using one, but he must then limit himself to furniture that does not require turned pieces such as balusters or shaped posts. Carving such miniature pieces by hand, especially if two or more must be the same, is very difficult for anyone but an experienced wood-carver.

The selection of lathes on the market which are capable of turning small wood pieces is very limited; and the wood lathes sold for home workshops are much too large for miniature work.

The problem that must be considered is the manner in which the wood stick or dowel (called a "workpiece") is to be mounted in the lathe for turning. In principle, a lathe is simply a motorized tool that supports and rotates the workpiece, which is then shaped by holding a cutting tool against it as it turns. The two ends of the workpiece must be supported at their exact centers or the workpiece will wobble as it turns, making accurate work impossible. Moreover, the left end must be gripped so that it can be rotated by the motor.

The right end of the workpiece is always supported by the point of a small metal piece (called a "lathe center") which is held in the right end of the lathe (called the "tailstock" of the lathe). To mount the right end of the workpiece is a simple matter and is discussed more fully in chapter 6.

However, to mount the left end of the workpiece in the left end of the lathe (called the "headstock" of the lathe) is a more complicated problem. There are several types of accessories on the market which can be used for this purpose, and a discussion of each follows:

1.   The left end of the wood workpiece can be mounted on a metal piece, called a "spur center." This consists of a center metal point around which are four sharp projections (spurs) that bite into the wood to hold it so it will rotate. To use a spur center, grooves into which the spurs will fit must be sawed or cut in the end of the workpiece. The spur center is fitted into the end of the motor shaft, or "spindle," and is rotated by the motor. Spur centers now available are too large to hold a workpiece less than ¼ inch in diameter.

2.   The left end of the workpiece can be fastened in a "lathe dog," shown in the illustration. Although primarily intended for use with metal, it can also be used to support a wood piece. The workpiece is secured in the collar of the dog which, in turn, is fitted to the spindle. Altogether, it is a cumbersome arrangement for use with small dowels which, in miniature work, may be no more than ⅛ inch in diameter.

3.   The most convenient method for supporting all small workpieces, wood or metal, is to use a chuck fitted to the spin-

Lathe dog.

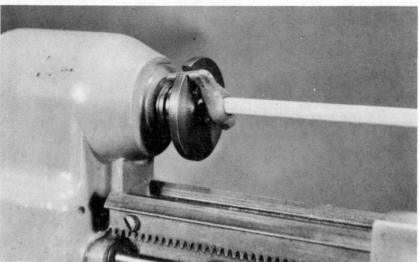

dle. A chuck is a hollow metal piece into which the end of the workpiece is inserted. There are then various methods for tightening the chuck around the workpiece to hold it firmly:

    a. A "collet" chuck, the least expensive, has a separate metal sleeve that fits inside the chuck and is squeezed around the workpiece end when the chuck is tightened. Each sleeve will hold a workpiece of only one diameter, but a collet chuck usually comes with three or four sleeves of assorted sizes.

    b. A "hand-tightening" chuck has three or four internal metal jaws that close around a workpiece end when the chuck is fastened to the spindle. This type will hold a workpiece of any diameter that can be inserted into it.

Hand-tightening chuck.

    c. A "key" chuck is the same as a hand-tightening chuck except that it is made in two parts and only the outer part need be turned to tighten the chuck around the workpiece. Tightening is done with a key (furnished with the chuck) which makes it easy to tighten the workpiece securely.

d.   A "4-jaw" chuck has four large jaws, each of which is moved separately by use of a furnished key. To center the workpiece, all jaws must be moved inward an equal distance, which is not always easy to accomplish. However, the chuck will hold both square and round workpieces.

4-jaw chuck.

e.   A "3-jaw" chuck is similar to the 4-jaw except that all three jaws are moved simultaneously by the key, and a round workpiece is centered automatically. Although it is the most expensive of the chucks mentioned here, it is an excellent type to use for small dowels.

As far as the writer has been able to learn, there are only three types of small lathes available for miniature work:

1.   A model maker's lathe is a precision instrument which, although intended for use with metal, can also be used for wood. It turns at a much slower speed than does a wood-turning lathe,

and this somewhat slows the work, but any of the above-mentioned chucks can be used with it, in addition to other accessories for special jobs. Because of its slow speed, it is almost impossible to use wood-turning chisels for shaping the workpiece, but since, for miniature work, narrow files and emery boards are more convenient to use, this is no drawback. The writer has used such a lathe for years with no handicap other than a negligible loss of time.

Model maker's metal lathe can be used for wood.

2. A small toolmaker's lathe is available which, although intended for turning metal, has a variable-speed motor which can be turned up for use with wood. A key chuck is purchased separately for supporting a wood workpiece. This is a well-made lathe and, although larger than the model maker's lathe, can be used successfully for miniature work.

3. A small, inexpensive, wood-turning lathe is designed for workpieces from ¼ inch to 1½ inch in diameter, and up to 6

inches long. Instructions that come with the lathe tell how a workpiece smaller than ¼ inch in diameter can be adapted for use in the lathe, but it is a complicated procedure which the craftsman, if he has a choice, would be wise to avoid.

The above types of lathes are generally available in hobby shops, some hardware and department stores, and through some mail-order catalogs.

Files

Within reason, the more small files of assorted shapes and grades the craftsman owns, the better. First in importance is an all-purpose flat file of medium grade, 6 to 8 inches long and ¹⁄₂ inch or so wide. This will be used mainly for straightening edges, for leveling small, flat areas and for making the legs of a piece exactly the same length. One or more of these operations will be necessary for nearly every piece of furniture that will be made.

Other, narrower files will have many uses including the shaping of turnings on a lathe, smoothing carvings, and shaping

The more small files, the better.

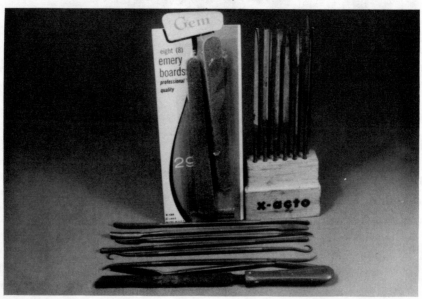

edges. Such files of many shapes and sizes can be bought separately or in sets. Among the many available are riffler files (often used in making jewelry), needle files and pin files (some as small as .050 inches in diameter). There are round files, triangular files, files with sharp cutting edges and mill files (flat on one side and rounded on the other). The list is almost endless.

If the craftsman starts with the flat file mentioned above, and one of the sets of small, shaped files, he will be adequately equipped. Others may be purchased later if the need arises.

Sandpaper

It would be impossible to make a successful piece of miniature furniture without at least one grade of sandpaper. Every piece of wood cut on a saw should be well sanded before anything else is done to it. Before staining, finished pieces should be sanded to smooth joints, straighten lines and remove all signs of small flaws in workmanship.

The sandpaper should range in grits from very fine to medium. Coarse sandpaper is seldom needed for miniature work. Any sandpaper bought should be of as good a quality as the craftsman can afford to buy, and this quality is usually found in large sheets rather than in assorted packs. Some such packs contain paper of such a cheap grade that the grit drops off as soon as pressure is applied. Small pieces of the better quality can be torn from the sheets as needed; scissors will be dulled if used for cutting sandpaper.

The craftsman will also find that a pack of emery boards will come in handy. These are available at most counters where nail polishes are sold. One side of an emery board is of a medium grit, the other of a finer one. Such boards can be used as slightly flexible files in some situations, as sandpaper in others, and, when cut into narrow strips, are useful for getting into small, hard-to-reach places. Emery boards are also useful as shaping tools in lathe work.

Clamps

A set of clamps of one kind or another is necessary when flat pieces are to be glued together. These may be either C-clamps with screws which tighten the wood pieces against each other, or simple spring paper clips which can be found in any dime store. Both types are shown in the illustration.

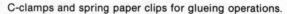

C-clamps and spring paper clips for glueing operations.

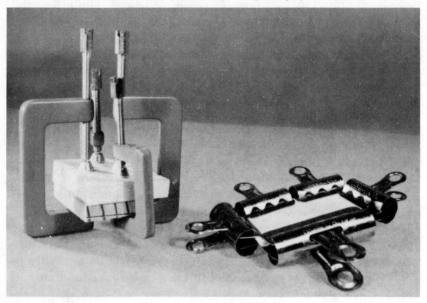

If the pieces to be glued are so thick that the paper clip type will not open wide enough, the C-clamps must be used. Otherwise, the paper clips cost less and are easier to use. Five or six clamps ranging in size from 1 inch to 2½ inches across should be sufficient to do any glueing job.

Soldering Iron

A soldering iron is necessary only if the craftsman wishes to work in metals, and the only requirement of such an iron is that it have a small tip—about the size of a thick pencil point. A small, electric soldering iron can be purchased separately, and interchangeable tips of assorted sizes usually come as a set, as shown here. Such irons and sets of tips are not expensive, and since they are much used in radio repair work, can usually be found in shops which sell radio parts.

A roll of soft solder (a heavy, silver-colored wire with a flux core) should be purchased at the same time.

Soldering equipment. Three tips are interchangeable in iron.

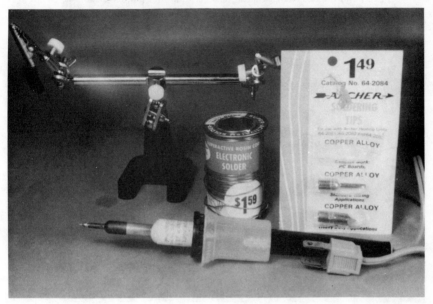

Glass Cutters

For cutting a straight-sided mirror or piece of glass, a good quality, diamond glass cutter will be needed. Curved glass edges require the use of a diamond pencil. Both tools are shown in the illustration. Although cutters with diamond points are more expensive than those which cut with steel wheels, they are far superior for miniature work, and will not become dull. Steel cutters can dull very quickly and are comparatively awkward to handle.

If the edges of the glass are to be smoothed and beveled, a grinding wheel will be needed. Since this is a special tool which will be needed for only one purpose, it is described more fully in chapter 11 in the section on cutting mirrors. If the craftsman does not have such a tool, he will probably not want to buy one for such limited use, but may know the owner of one who will allow him to use it for the short time it will take to polish and bevel the edges of a few small mirrors.

Diamond glass cutter for straight cuts, diamond pencil for curves.

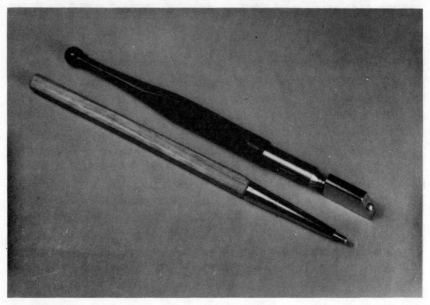

Miscellaneous

Anyone who enjoys working with his hands will know that a detailed list of every small tool he will accumulate as he goes along would be useless. He will acquire them, one by one, as the need arises. If a particular job calls for curved brass wire, for example, he will need a wire cutter and a pair of wire-bending pliers. If he is using small screws, a tiny screwdriver will come in handy, although the tip of a knife will do. A few Exacto blades will be useful for shaving dowels from toothpicks (the handles are not necessary for small work). A miniature hand saw, only a few inches long, will make setting up the jigsaw unnecessary when only a narrow piece of wood needs to be cut in two. A small vise will also come in handy at times, but it is not indispensable.

3

Materials

The reader who has never liked to throw anything away will enjoy this chapter. It will justify the instinct he has had all along to save everything, no matter how small and seemingly useless, for what worse fate than to find that the very thing that would have put the finishing touch to a particular miniature piece was discarded a while back?

Old jewelry of all kinds is pure gold to the maker of miniatures. Delicate, filigree pieces are especially useful, since small pieces can be snipped from them to make such things as drawer pulls, keyhole escutcheons, and doorknobs. Chain links of appropriate shapes can fill the same purposes, and the rest of the chain used to hang a chandelier. Watches that no longer run yield dials, thin wheels, and many odd-shaped pieces that will suggest their own uses as needs arise.

It is sometimes difficult to find material for upholstery, bedspreads, and curtains—material that is of a weave and pattern fine enough to be in correct proportion to the scale (and the careful craftsman will use no other). When such a piece is found by chance in a store, even if there is no immediate need

Now there is an excuse for saving almost anything.

For the sewing machine, an old watch furnished the wheels, threading hardware, and spool and needle holders.

for it, ⅛ or ¼ yard should be bought and put away for future use. Discarded neckties with very small patterns also make excellent upholstery material, and appropriate ones should be saved for the purpose.

Fine, delicate lace, also difficult to find, should be saved for future needs. If the pattern is right, a small center square or circle can be used as a doily or an antimacassar, and the edges for trim on curtains and pillowcases.

Small mirrors are not as plentiful as they were once. They no longer come as standard equipment in purses and cosmetic cases but are still included in compacts. If no-longer-used mirrors cannot be found around the house, asking friends to save their small mirrors in the future will usually bring in a good supply.

Pieces of thin glass and of heavy, clear plastic will come in handy. The plastic can be used to cover framed pictures or to substitute for glass in small or curved doors; the glass can be used in larger doors and windows.

In addition to the odds and ends already on hand, the purchase of a few small, inexpensive items will greatly simplify the making of miniatures. Toothpicks, both round and flat, have many uses. To name a few such uses, the round ones can become stretchers and spindles for some chair styles such as Windsor or colonial. The flat ones are excellent for mixing small amounts of paints, stains, and epoxy, and for applying adhesives. Toothpicks make handy, pointed tools for cleaning out small cracks and crevices in furniture without scratching the wood, and for wiping away excess adhesives during a glueing operation. Sanded to an even thickness, the tips of toothpicks can be used as dowels to strengthen glued joints.

A box of brass pins, found in dime stores or notion departments, is almost a necessity. The heads can be used for decorative studs on an upholstered chair or footstool. With the head removed, the pin becomes a useful, straight rod. Cut short and pushed into drilled holes, brass pins can be used as tacks or brads, or for fastening pulls and knobs to drawers and doors.

Most hobby shops, and those which specialize in model train supplies in particular, carry a selection of thin brass or aluminum rods, and of tubes, both round and square, some of which nest into the next larger sizes. In the same shops are sheets of brass of assorted thicknesses, some so thin they can be cut with scissors, and fine brass filigree pieces (used on the observation cars of model trains) which can be used as trim on picture and mirror frames and on some styles of furniture.

It would be impossible to list all the bits and pieces that might be of use to the craftsman. Such a list, moreover, would deprive him of the challenge of using his own imagination as he goes along. He should be reminded again, however, that he is not making toys. The original purpose of whatever pieces are used in the making of miniatures should not be recognized as such. "Cute" ideas should be saved for dollhouses and not used in carefully furnished miniature rooms.

Polyform

Among the craftsman's supplies should be kept a pound of a claylike material, sold under the names of "Polyform" or "Sculpey." It is an amazingly versatile product. Polyform is not

Polyform—a versatile product for workers in miniature.

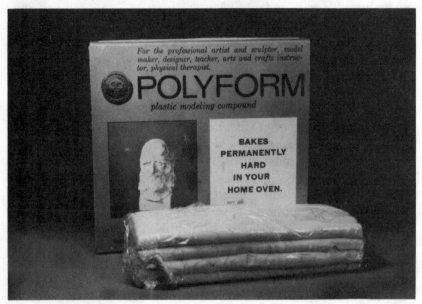

sticky, can be molded into fine details, will not shrink when hardened in a slow oven for fifteen or twenty minutes, and can be kept indefinitely on the shelf without drying out. It is a white substance that does not change color when baked for the recommended period, but gradually darkens with longer baking. If left for many hours in the oven, it will turn a dark slate color, but is otherwise unharmed. After baking, it can be sawed, sanded, and painted.

The writer has used Polyform for making bowls, plates, clock cases, flowers, doll heads and toys, statuary, and lamp bases among other things. It has been used to make stones and bricks for fireplaces and as mortar for laying them. Trim has been made of it for decorating mirror and picture frames. Elaborate pieces have been made in stages and baked between each stage. Vines and leaves have been added to a wood post and, when baked and painted to match the wood, appear to be fine carving which could not possibly have been done by hand. To give it the appearance of porcelain, baked Polyform has been painted with

For the "whatnot" shelf, tiny objects molded of Polyform.

water colors and a fine brush, then given a coat of clear nail polish.

In case such enthusiasm for a product should be misunderstood, the writer has no knowledge of the company which manufactures it. It is simply an excellent and easy-to-use material which fills many needs in miniature work. If it cannot be purchased locally, usually at an art-supply store, the reader can write to Polyform Products Company, 9420 Byron Street, Schiller Park, Illinois 60176, to learn the name of his nearest dealer.

Wood

Wood is the most important single material the craftsman will use in making miniature furniture. There are just three classes of wood with which he will work: plywood, softwood, and hardwood.

Although the three are discussed separately here, the division between hardwood and softwood is more a matter of terminology than of actual hardness of woods. Wood from a deciduous tree, such as an oak, elm, or maple, is porous and referred to as "hard." Conifers, such as pines, firs, and cedars, yield nonporous, "soft" wood. If the division were based only on the actual density of wood, however, there would be an intermingling of the two groups. Some species of hardwood trees yield fairly soft wood, while some softwoods are comparatively hard.

Plywood

Plywood is composed of three layers of wood (usually soft), with the grain of the center layer running crosswise to the two outer layers which run in the same direction. This arrangement makes the wood much stronger than would be a single layer of the same thickness.

It does not, however, make plywood equally strong in both directions. As with any other wood, the grain of the outer layers of plywood should run with the length of a cut piece. Cutting with and against the grain is discussed more fully in chapter 5.

Plywood is an easy wood to cut accurately. It will not split and is much less apt to break than other woods when cut in very narrow strips. In addition, the thickness of plywood is constant throughout the whole piece. The thickness of a single, thin slice, cut from a block of any other wood, may vary slightly in places, and these variations must be watched for and used where they will not show.

When used for miniature furniture, however, plywood has two shortcomings. The first is that its soft wood will not take an excellent finish. This is not such a serious handicap, however, that plywood should be eliminated from the list of usable woods. With a little extra care, all but large, unbroken areas (such as a dining table top) can be given a very acceptable finish.

The second shortcoming is that plywood edges, if more than $\frac{1}{32}$ inch thick, and if exposed in the furniture, will show the separate layers. This drawback can also be overcome. The edges of pieces $\frac{1}{16}$ inch thick can be rounded off by sanding so the layers will not be noticed. Edges of pieces thicker than $\frac{1}{16}$ should be concealed with narrow strips of wood as explained in chapter 9. Plywood edges were covered with wood strips on the apron of the oval table shown in that chapter and the curved side pieces of the desk front shown in chapter 1. Both of these pieces are made entirely of plywood.

Easily obtained in hobby shops and many other stores, plywood comes in convenient-sized sheets, in thicknesses of $\frac{1}{32}$ inch, $\frac{1}{16}$ inch, $\frac{3}{32}$ inch, $\frac{1}{8}$ inch, and $\frac{1}{4}$ inch. No other wood is offered in such a complete range of thicknesses.

Although not usually so labeled, the outer layers of most plywood are made of pine, but when the layers are made of balsa, they are usually marked as such. Balsa is an excellent wood for special purposes but should not be used for cabinetwork.

It is recommended that the craftsman use plywood for his first piece of furniture, not only because of the ease with which it can be worked, but also because it is comparatively inexpensive. If that first piece does not turn out to be as successful as a later one, it can be discarded with a clear conscience.

Softwood

Although hardwood is preferable for making both full-size and miniature furniture, a selection of softwood will come in handy. Like plywood, softwood is easily obtainable in thin pieces, although not always in the thickness needed for a particular job. Stores which carry model train supplies usually offer a variety of the more popular softwoods such as pine, spruce, basswood, and balsa.

These can be used in many ways. To save more expensive and harder-to-find hardwoods, softwood can be used for the backs and bottoms of furniture, for drawers and for any parts that will not show in the finished piece. Either plywood or softwood is needed as a supporting piece when cutting thin or very small pieces as explained in chapter 5 on sawing. It is also useful for practice and for testing the fit of patterns the craftsman may originate.

Since it is comparatively easy to shape by hand-sanding, long hours of tedious work can be avoided by using softwood for small parts of miniature furniture which need special shaping. When it has been carefully stained and finished, softwood used for such small parts will not be noticeably different from the hardwood used for the rest of the furniture.

For a larger piece that is to be elaborately shaped by sanding, balsa is an excellent wood to use. It is such soft, light material that care must be taken not to sand too vigorously or, before the craftsman realizes it, more wood will have been taken off than was intended. Balsa should be used only when soft edges and curves are wanted, since it will not hold sharp corners or points. The wood will not take an acceptable stain finish and should be used only when it is to be painted.

Hardwood

Whenever possible, hardwood should be used for most miniature furniture. It can be sawed into fine details with little danger of small points and thin edges breaking off, and most important, it takes a beautiful finish with very little work. Stains penetrate the wood evenly, and while softwoods may need a finishing coat of varnish or similar material, a coat of wax over the stain is usually all that is needed to give hardwood a smooth, rich finish.

Through the centuries exotic and rare woods have been used for occasional pieces of furniture; but the qualities of a few such woods have proven to be so desirable, they are now used in manufactured furniture almost to the exclusion of all the rest. The most popular of these hardwoods are oak, mahogany, walnut, rosewood, maple, cherry and some of the other fruit-woods.

Although hardwood is not as widely sold as are softwood and plywood, finding sufficient supplies of it is not difficult. In most cities there is at least one company which specializes in hard-woods, and companies who sell it by mail advertise widely in magazines and, in particular, hobby and do-it-yourself publications. While it costs more than other woods, the cost of hard-wood, in small pieces, is not prohibitive.

For hardwood that costs nothing at all, there are the trees in one's own yard. While it is not recommended that the shape of a beautiful tree be marred by removing a branch for the sake of obtaining wood, there are times when necessary pruning, or a heavy storm, will make limbs available which are thick enough for drying and slicing.

The wood can be kiln-dried at home by baking it in a slow oven to remove the moisture. The oven temperature should be set above the boiling point of water, which is 212 degrees Fahrenheit, but not so high that the wood will burn. Home ovens are not always accurate, but if the temperature is kept between 220 and 240 degrees, the wood will dry satisfactorily.

To be technically correct, the wood should be weighed on an analytical scale from time to time as it is being baked. When it shows no more weight loss, it is completely dry and ready for use. Such precision is not necessary, however, and usually not possible, when a home oven is being used. Woods vary in moisture content, but any branch, two to four inches thick, should be completely dry if left in a heated oven twelve to twenty-four hours. The total baking period may be broken into two or three shorter ones if it is more convenient to do so.

The illustration shows a section of a magnolia branch after it has been oven-dried in the above manner, as well as the ready-to-use wood slices that were taken from it. Magnolia wood is one of the few hardwoods to come from an evergreen tree, and while it is not one of the more popular furniture woods, this was a case of "any tree in a storm" which made it available.

Magnolia branch, dried in home oven and sliced, ready for use.

Although the foregoing discussion of hardwood sources paints a rosy picture for the craftsman, there is a catch. As far as the writer has been able to learn, ready-cut hardwoods cannot be bought in a selection of thicknesses suitable for miniature work. Veneers, in thicknesses ranging from $\frac{1}{28}$ to $\frac{1}{40}$ inch are made of the most popular hardwoods, and while these are very useful when used in combination with thicker pieces of matching wood, whole pieces of furniture cannot be made of veneer alone.

Since an interest in making miniature furniture is becoming so widespread, sooner or later some enterprising company will probably offer hardwoods in suitable thicknesses. Until then the only solution seems to be that the craftsman slice his own. If he does not have the necessary tools, he may know someone who does, or he can go to a professional woodworking shop where the wood can be cut for him.

A wood block 2 x 4 x 6 inches is the ideal size with which to start, although blocks 2 to 3 inches thick by 3 to 8 inches wide, and in any convenient length, will serve the purpose. Sizes such as these are listed as "carving blocks" in most catalogs.

Since a circular saw will waste too much wood, a thin-bladed band saw will be needed. The saw illustrated is a 12-inch tool fitted with a fence and a ½-inch wood-cutting blade. In addition, although the wood slices can be hand-sanded to the required thickness and smoothness, much time and effort can be saved if the craftsman has access to a 6-inch belt sander.

To start, one side of the block should be squared lengthwise so that it forms an exact right angle with the bottom of the block. The bottom should then be so marked with a pencil and, during sawing, should always be placed down against the saw's table. After the side has been squared with the bottom, it should be sanded with the grain until it is flat, straight, and smooth. If a belt sander is used, the fence should be installed at an accurate right angle to the table top. The block is then held lightly against the belt and fence until the sanding has been done. No pressure should be given; the weight of the block will supply all the pressure needed.

The block is now ready for slicing. The band-saw fence should be adjusted so that its distance from the blade equals the thickness of the slice wanted, plus about $\frac{1}{64}$ inch to allow for later sanding. The side of the fence must form an exact right angle to the tabletop, and the fence, end-to-end, must be exactly parallel to the blade.

With the saw running, the wood block is then fed to the blade by holding it firmly against the fence and moving it in steadily, as fast as the blade will cut it freely. After each slice is cut, the block should again be sanded smooth. In this way, one side of each slice will be finished and ready to use before it is cut from the block.

Cutting thin wood slices.

Using the above method, slices of fine-grain hardwood can be cut as thin as ⅟₃₂ inch. Coarse-grain wood or softwood is a little more difficult to cut this thin.

In most cases it is not necessary to sand the second side of each slice but, if needed, it can be sanded by hand by wrapping a piece of medium-grit sandpaper around a flat board a little larger than the hardwood slice. Doing the work with a belt sander will save time but, since the wood slice is so thin, great care must be taken not to burn the fingers. The slice should be

Block face is sanded smooth after each cut.

kept in motion with first one end, then the other, being sanded. Progress should be checked frequently. Pressure against the belt should be very light to prevent the belt from "grabbing" the wood and injuring the fingers.

Once the band saw and sander have been set up for cutting and smoothing thin slices of wood, it is a good idea to stay with the work and prepare as many pieces as possible. To the maker of miniature furniture, nothing could be more satisfying than an ample supply of thin, ready-to-use pieces of beautiful hardwood.

4

Planning the Work

Before the actual work of making furniture is begun, there is some important planning to be done. As eager as the craftsman may be to start sawing, sanding, and glueing, he will save both time and material if he has an accurate pattern to follow and a good idea in advance of how a certain piece should be constructed.

The craftsman should first decide what scale to use. It is an important decision because once taken, the same scale should be used for all the furniture he will make.

Choosing a Scale

The term "miniature furniture" can mean almost anything. Over the years, craftsmen have been reproducing full-size furniture in sizes large enough for children to use down to those useful only as toys or for display. All of it can correctly be called "miniature." The difference is in the scale.

If a 6-foot sofa, for example, were reproduced in a 2-foot copy, the scale used would have been 1 foot to 3 feet. If a 3-inch copy had been made of the same sofa, the scale would have been ½ inch to 1 foot.

Although the reader may choose any scale he prefers, a ratio of 1 inch to 1 foot is most often used for miniature furniture. Second in popularity (although far down the line) is a ¾-inch to 1-foot scale. Using these scales, the 6-foot sofa would be reduced to 6 inches and 4½ inches, respectively.

The 1-inch to 1-foot scale has two major advantages. First, it is the one used for nearly all of the miniature furniture and accessories sold commercially. Although the craftsman's own furniture will be superior to manufactured pieces, accessories of metal and glass, most of which he is not equipped to make, will be welcome additions to his rooms.

Doorknobs, drawer pulls, face plates and hinges, to name a few, are nearly all manufactured on the 1-inch scale. While some of these are not of a good quality, others are, and it is a great advantage to be able to use them.

The second advantage is that, within limits, the larger the piece, the easier it is to make. Furniture made on the 1-inch scale is approximately ⅓ larger than that for which the ¾-inch scale is used, and the difference is enough to make fine detail work a little easier to execute.

The 1-inch scale has one disadvantage. When planning a miniature replica, exact measurements on the pattern are most important. On this scale, a measurement on the full-size model of 2 inches would be reduced to ⅙ inch, a 5-inch measurement to ⁵⁄₁₂ inch. A study of the conversion table at the end of this chapter will give the reader an idea of how measurements run on each of the two scales.

Nearly all rulers are marked with 16 spaces to an inch, and a linear inch on most graph paper contains either 4 or 8 spaces. These divisions are correct for measurements on the ¾-inch to 1-foot scale. The two measurements mentioned above of ⅙ and ⁵⁄₁₂ inches would have to be estimated, and while this can be done with reasonable accuracy, it does make the work of fitting pieces together somewhat more difficult.

Although it is true that when using the 1-inch scale, full-size measurements that come out on even feet are transposed to even inches on the table, in practice most measurements will be in inches rather than feet, and it is the inches, and fractions of inches, that will have to be estimated. The problem can be solved, of course, if rulers marked with 12 spaces to an inch, and graph paper with 6 or 12 spaces to a linear inch, can be found. Such rulers and paper are made, but are difficult to find.

The disadvantages of using the ¾-inch scale have already been mentioned. In the matter of accessories, however, many pieces that are manufactured on the 1-inch scale are suitable for use with the smaller-size furniture. A 1-inch vase, for example, on a table made on the 1-inch scale, would represent a vase 1 foot high. The same vase on a ¾-inch scale table, if full size, would be 15 inches high. Since neither height is out of line for a vase, it could be used on either table.

The same accessories can be used on tables built on different scales.

The same holds true for other accessories which vary in sizes. Chandeliers, lamps, picture frames, trays, mirrors, and decorative bowls are a few examples. Some other items, however, are not interchangeable on the two scales. For instance, all eyeglasses are pretty much the same size, as are table flatware, dinner plates, spools of thread, newspapers, phonograph records, and so on.

The advantages of the ¾-inch scale are two, the most important of which is the ease of measurements which has already been discussed. The second is the matter of available space in the craftsman's home. If it is limited, and if a number of miniature rooms are to be displayed, about a third less space will be required if the ¾-inch scale is used. A 20-foot room built on the 1-inch scale would be 20 inches long, but only 15 on the smaller scale.

For the two reasons mentioned, the writer prefers the ¾-inch scale (used for all the furniture shown in this book), but she is in the minority. It is purely a matter of personal preference, and the craftsman should make his own choice.

Planning Construction

One of the most important, and most enjoyable, steps in making miniature replicas is planning the construction of a piece and figuring out how to copy some unusual feature. Often, very elaborate features can easily be duplicated, while those which attract little attention may need to be considered carefully before the work is started.

The sideboard shown in the illustration is an example. If the reader were asked to guess which of its parts were most difficult to plan, the answers would probably include the carving, the beveled mirrors, and the turned posts. However, the methods used for making these things are more-or-less standard and are covered in this book.

The angle at which the corner posts of the base are turned is the detail which required the most planning beforehand. It is a feature that is hardly noticed and would not have been missed if omitted, but it does add to the effectiveness of the whole piece. The craftsman, considering a full-size piece to reproduce, might glance at this sideboard and think, as the writer did at first, "That looks easy. Just glue the posts on at an angle." But if this were done, how could the doors be opened against a slanted jamb? How should the sides be fastened to the posts? What about the corners of the top, under the marble? Obviously, the

Ornate sideboard, 5 inches high, presented a special problem.

edges of all pieces that were to be glued to the posts would have to be beveled, but at what angle?

Similar questions will arise with regard to other pieces the craftsman might be considering. If the upholstery of a chair or sofa is tufted, how could it be done? Would the same piece look as well with a different upholstery? There are shell carvings on the knees of the cabriole legs. Could they be included in the copy and if so, how? The frame of the back of a Victorian chair has a two-dimensional curve that sweeps forward and down to become the arms. How could such a curve be made, could it be omitted, or would it be wiser to choose some other piece to make?

That particular curve is a characteristic of much Victorian furniture. If the curving armrest is omitted from a chair origi-nally designed for its use, the whole character of the piece

would be lost. Similarly, the craftsman is not likely to improve
the classic lines of a Duncan Phyfe pedestal table, or the intricate
inside cuts of a Chinese Chippendale chair, by simplifying them.
Therefore, if he cannot picture in advance how such work can
be handled, he would be wiser to select some other piece whose
construction is clearer.

There is nothing wrong, however, in changing a design if
there is good reason for it. Designers of mass-produced furniture
had to consider cost as well as appearance, and unless historical
accuracy is important to the craftsman, there is no reason why
he should not add more details or improve the lines of such
pieces. These changes should be made judiciously, however, and
only to improve the design, not to make the work easier.

Measuring

If the piece of furniture that has been selected for reproduction is
available for measuring, accurate measurements can easily be
obtained. However, if it is necessary to work from a picture,
dimensions that are not given will have to be estimated. This can
be done by taking the most important measurements, such as the
height and width of a piece, from furniture of the same general
style in one's own home. The distances from all chair seats to the
floor are pretty much the same. Dining tables are usually the
same general height, as are most beds. If one reasonably accurate measurement can be obtained, the rest can be closely
estimated by studying the proportions of the piece to be copied.
For example, if a wardrobe is 6 feet high, the picture itself can
be measured to learn the ratio between its height and width. The
exact height and width of a piece is not as important as the relationship between the two and between all the parts.

Even more important is that exact measurements be kept
when drawing the pattern. If an estimate of the height of the
model is off an inch or so, it does not matter. However, if a part
drawn on the pattern is off even $\frac{1}{32}$ inch, it will not fit with the
rest of the parts if they have been drawn accurately. Therefore,
although careful measurements are important in every phase of
the work, it is crucial that the pattern be exact.

The relationship between height and width is more important than exact measurements.

When taking or estimating measurements, it is not necessary to include every detail of a piece such as trim, edging strips and so on. Only the dimensions of major parts (panels, doors, openings for drawers, legs, seats and backs, for example) need be considered. Using the conversion table, the measurements taken are then converted to the correct matching figures for whichever scale is being used.

Although every fraction of an inch is not included in the table, it is not difficult to obtain any dimension needed by adding together the correct figures. For example, if a full-size measurement is ¾ inch and the 1-inch scale is being used, figures would be taken from the table for ½- and ¼-inch measurements which would be $\frac{1}{24}$ inch and $\frac{1}{48}$ inch, respectively. The total of these two is $\frac{1}{16}$ inch—the correct measurement.

Using the dimensions obtained from the table for the miniature piece, simple front and side view drawings are then drawn on graph paper. These drawings will be left untouched until the piece is finished and will be used as guides for making patterns of the individual parts as they are needed.

There is one point to consider before the drawing is completed. The stock of wood the craftsman has on hand may not include a piece of the exact thickness needed. If the difference is not enough to be noticed, but is enough to affect the construction of the piece, the drawing should be adjusted to take into account the thickness of the wood piece that will be used.

Where construction will not be affected, as in the case of a tabletop, the exact thickness of the wood used will not matter as long as it looks proportionally correct. If the only piece available for the top is obviously too thick, it should not be used at all. If it is too thin, however, it can be combined with another piece to approximate the correct measurement and the drawing made according to this measurement.

Tabletop may be made of several layers if available wood is too thin.

A typical pattern drawing is shown in the illustration. The advertisement for the Roman chair was first published in the 1897 catalog of Montgomery Ward. When the pattern for this chair was being planned, it appeared at first glance that the upper and lower curves were identical arcs of circles. However, closer examination showed that the upper curves were somewhat flattened to make the chair more comfortable. The legs were therefore drawn with a compass and the upper section by hand.

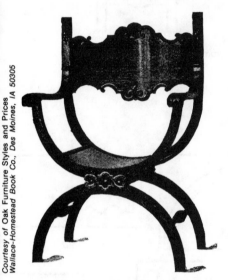 

Courtesy of Oak Furniture Styles and Prices
Wallace-Homestead Book Co., Des Moines, IA 50305

Roman chair was copied from an advertisement originally in an 1897 Montgomery Ward catalog.

Patterns for the separate pieces were then drawn as shown. In order to make the upper curves and the elaborate shape of the splat perfectly symmetrical, only half patterns were drawn for these pieces. The paper was folded along the center line of each drawing, a few dabs of rubber cement were added on the inside edges to keep the two halves from slipping, and the pattern was cut out with scissors.

Where two identical pieces were needed, only one pattern was

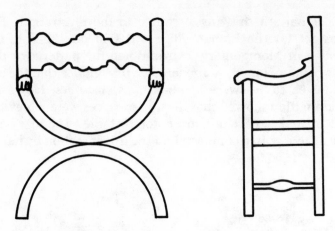

Front and side views of Roman chair.

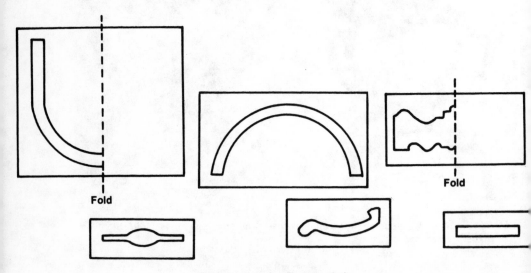

Pattern parts for Roman chair.

drawn as shown. Following the method described in chapter 5, each pair was then sawed in one operation, after which the ends of the upper front curve were shortened to the correct height for the arms.

Since the seat had a deep curve in it which would have been

difficult to shape from the rosewood used for the rest of the chair, and since this seat would later be upholstered in leather, a block of balsa was used for which no pattern was needed. This was easily sanded and filed to the correct shape and size.

A few changes were made in the design. The height was reduced, the splat was narrowed a little, and although no trim was omitted, some of it was slightly altered.

This chair was fairly simple to make. When planning a more complicated piece, however, it is not necessary, nor always wise, to draw all the pattern parts at one time. When making a sideboard, for example, which is divided into an upper and lower section, the whole piece should be drawn on graph paper as described. It would then be safer to draw patterns for the lower section only. When these pieces have been sawed and glued together, measurements can be checked. This will serve to correct any slight errors that might have been made in the base, and will also ensure the correct fit of the upper and lower sections.

Each paper pattern is cut separately from the sheet and fastened to the wood with rubber cement. Since it is easier to follow lines with a saw blade when there is a white background, a margin of about $\frac{1}{8}$ inch should be left around each drawing. For reasons of economy, margins can be removed from a corner or straight edge of a pattern if a corner or edge of the wood can be used for these lines. In such a case, the pattern is glued right up to the edge of the wood.

Almost without exception, fastening a paper pattern to the wood is far better than drawing lines on the wood itself. Pencil lines on dark wood are hard to see clearly, they cannot be drawn as fine as the lines on graph paper, and the advantage of the mechanically perfect printed lines would be lost if the pattern had to be redrawn on the wood. Neither is drawing around a pattern a satisfactory method. It cannot be done with complete accuracy. If only a straight strip is needed, however, it may be drawn on the wood, using a sharp pencil and ruler.

When two or more pieces must be the same shape and cannot be cut in a single operation, identical patterns should be made. If these patterns consist only of straight lines, it is easy to draw as many as needed using just graph paper and ruler. However, if the lines are curved, making two drawings exactly alike is more difficult than it may sound even if graph paper is used. To make such patterns, small pieces of both graph paper and carbon paper, a little larger than the drawing, are cut and stacked alternately with the graph paper on top and the carbons face down. A little rubber cement is then spread along two edges of the stack to keep the papers from slipping. The drawing is next traced heavily on the top piece of paper and the stack separated by cutting off the glued edges.

If all the talk of fractions and accurate dimensions in this chapter have intimidated the reader, a word of assurance should be added here. Some things are far more frightening in print than in practice, and numbers are among the worst offenders. A strip of wood $1/16$ inch wide is not a fraction but a narrow strip of wood, and once the work is started, numbers on paper will fall into their proper perspective as useful things, and not as tyrants.

Conversion Table

Full-Size Measurements	1" to 1' Scale	3/4" to 1' Scale
$1/4$"	$1/48$"	$1/64$"
$1/2$"	$1/24$"	$1/32$"
1"	$1/12$"	$1/16$"
1 $1/2$"	$1/8$"	$3/32$"
2"	$1/6$"	$1/8$"
2 $1/2$"	$5/24$"	$5/32$"
3"	$1/4$"	$3/16$"
3 $1/2$"	$7/24$"	$7/32$"
4"	$1/3$"	$1/4$"
4 $1/2$"	$9/24$"	$9/32$"
5"	$5/12$"	$5/16$"
5 $1/2$"	$11/24$"	$11/32$"
6"	$1/2$"	$3/8$"
6 $1/2$"	$13/24$"	$13/32$"

Full-Size Measurements	1″ to 1′ Scale	¾″ to 1′ Scale
7″	$\frac{7}{12}$″	$\frac{7}{16}$″
7 ½″	$\frac{15}{24}$″	$\frac{15}{32}$″
8″	$\frac{2}{3}$″	½″
8 ½″	$\frac{17}{24}$″	$\frac{17}{32}$″
9″	¾″	$\frac{9}{16}$″
9 ½″	$\frac{19}{24}$″	$\frac{19}{32}$″
10″	$\frac{5}{6}$″	⅝″
10 ½″	$\frac{21}{24}$″	$\frac{21}{32}$″
11″	$\frac{11}{12}$″	$\frac{11}{16}$″
11 ½″	$\frac{23}{24}$″	$\frac{23}{32}$″
1′	1″	¾″
1 ½′	1 ½″	1 ⅛″
2′	2″	1 ½″
2 ½′	2 ½″	1 ⅞″
3′	3″	2 ¼″
3 ½′	3 ½″	2 ⅝″
4′	4″	3″
4 ½′	4 ½″	3 ⅜″
5′	5″	3 ¾″
5 ½′	5 ½″	4 ⅛″
6′	6″	4 ½″
6 ½′	6 ½″	4 ⅞″
7′	7″	5 ¼″
7 ½′	7 ½″	5 ⅝″
8′	8″	6″
8 ½′	8 ½″	6 ⅜″
9′	9″	6 ¾″
9 ½′	9 ½″	7 ⅛″
10′	10″	7 ½″

5

Using the Jigsaw

Although learning to use a jigsaw takes only a few minutes, learning to use it skillfully will take a little longer. It is an uncomplicated tool, but so versatile it can do as simple or as complicated a job as the craftsman wishes. A good jigsaw will cut any wood, hard or soft, and in thicknesses up to two inches, although, for making miniature furniture, it is not likely that such thick wood will ever need to be cut.

The owner may have already set up his new saw, tried it out on a scrap of wood, and found that the blade was not cutting the wood at all. If so, he has made the common mistake of putting the blade in upside down. In order to cut into the wood, the teeth of the blade must be pointing downward.

When operating a jigsaw, there are only a few rules to follow. The tool should be placed on a level, flat surface and, unless there are suction cups on the feet of the tool, on a surface that is not slick.

Unless the saw is equipped with a presser foot, the return cycle of the blade has a tendency to pull the wood upward, away from the saw's table. This causes the wood to bounce up and down with the movement of the blade. It is therefore necessary to press the wood down firmly against the table as the work progresses.

Speed in sawing is not necessary—but accuracy is. Except for short straight cuts, the wood should be fed in very slowly and carefully. When making an intricate cut, it is a good idea to stop occasionally to examine the work already done and to plan the rest of it. During such pauses, the saw does not need to be turned off if the wood is held firmly in place. When sawing is resumed, the blade will start cutting at the exact point at which it stopped.

When starting a first cut, logic may dictate that in order to saw a line parallel to the edges of the wood, the wood should be held at a right angle to the blade and pushed straight forward. This is not always the case, however. The blade of a jigsaw is quite flexible, and if the wood used is a fairly thick piece of hardwood, its pressure against the blade may push the blade out of line. In such a case, in order to cut a straight line, the wood must be pushed in at a slight angle. For this reason, the eye cannot be trusted as the only guide to making an accurate cut. Lines to be sawed should be drawn on the wood itself, or on paper pasted to the wood.

The chances are that the new owner's first cut will not be a successful one. The blade will move so quickly and seem to be so eager to do the job, he may find himself feeding the wood in too fast and holding it too loosely against the table. His second and third cuts, however, will be noticeably better.

A little practice is far more important than following rules. The learner should draw some straight lines and wide curves on pieces of wood not more than ⅛ inch thick and try to cut them. When he is consistently able to hold the blade on the lines, he is ready to try something a little more complicated.

Cutting Sharp Curves and Angles
Since a jigsaw blade is thin and flexible, it can perform delicate operations as no other blade can. There is a limit, however, to what it can do. It cannot turn corners or follow sharp curves in one, single, unbroken operation.

These sharp turns are sawed by approaching them from more than one direction. In order to do this, the wood is cut to a certain point, then pulled back out of the saw and entered at another spot on the edge. The work slips out of the saw very easily if the motor is left running and the wood is turned as it comes so that the blade always stays in the line already cut.

Figure 1 illustrates how right angles should be sawed. If one should attempt to cut a right angle in a single operation, the corner would be rounded off and the sharp turn might cause the blade to break.

Figure 1

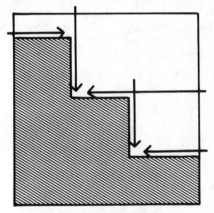

Sawing right angles.

Figure 2 shows a more complicated pattern. The first cut is made from 1 to A. The wood is then pulled out backwards, entered at point 2, and the second cut is made to B. The work is pulled out of the saw again and the next cut made from 3 to C. The fourth cut is made from 4 to C.

Figure 2

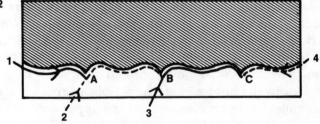

Sawing an elaborate edge.

Figure 3 shows a modified inside cut. The first cut is made from 1 to A, the second from 2 to B, the third from 3 to B, and the fourth from 4 to C. Unless the sawing has been very accurate, slight protrusions of wood may be left at points A and C. However, these can very easily be sanded off.

Figure 3

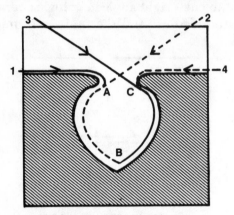

Making a modified inside cut.

The illustrated methods of handling several cuts are only suggestions. In sawing an intricate line with sharp turns or deep curves there are no set rules to follow but the principle must be understood. As the work progresses, the operator will be able to see how far he can go with one cut, and where he must back out and come in again from another angle.

Inside Cuts

An inside cut is simply a cut to which there is no outside entry for the blade. The area inside a frame, for example, would be removed with an inside cut. Almost without exception, an inside cut should be made before the outside shape of a piece is sawed.

To make such a cut, a hole is drilled or made with a sharp, pointed tool in the approximate center of the area to be sawed. The hole must be slightly larger than the upper end of the blade which is considerably wider than the blade itself.

The upper end of the blade is then disconnected from the saw

Courtesy of Oak Furniture Styles and Prices
Wallace-Homestead Book Co., Des Moines, IA 50305

Four inside cuts were needed for this hall tree, originally shown in an 1897 Montgomery Ward catalog.

and fed through the hole in the wood as shown. The wood **is** slipped down the blade to rest on the saw's table and the blade **is** reconnected to the saw at the top. The piece is now ready to cut.

Preparing for an inside cut.

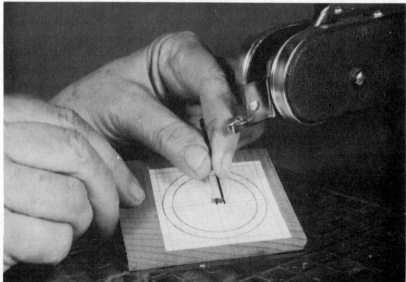

During the process, the blade should be held with an upward pull so that the lower end will not also become disconnected. If this should happen, however, no harm will have been done. The lower end will simply have to be replaced in its notch. When the cutting has been completed, the wood is removed from the saw by using the same procedure in reverse that was used to put it in.

An inside cut is seldom made in one continuous operation. The space in which to work is usually small and, in the case of a frame, there are four sharp corners to be sawed. Therefore, the method of cutting part of a line, then backing up and starting from another angle is nearly always used.

The inside cut is started in center hole.

At the start of the sawing, the hole that was made for the blade is all the space the operator has in which to work. If the first two cuts are made as shown in the illustration, however, a piece of wood will be released and from then on he will have all the room he needs in which to manipulate the blade. The first cut A is made from the hole to the corner. The wood is pulled back until the blade is again in the hole. The work is then turned, and cut B is made in a sweeping curve that joins the straight edge smoothly. The rest of the cut is a straight line to the corner.

Inside cuts can be made in any shape and of almost any size. It is possible to make one that is barely larger than the hole that was made for the blade. In this case, with such a small amount of wood to be cut away, the blade is used to smooth the edges rather than to saw into the wood. The edge to be smoothed is held at a right angle to the blade and moved carefully from side to side with the blade's teeth barely touching it. The blade then becomes more of a motorized file than a sawing instrument.

This same method of doing away with very tiny amounts of unwanted wood can be used for intricate outside cuts as well. If the desired shaping of any edge, inside or out, is so small the blade cannot saw it, it can be "filed" away as described above.

Sawing With and Against the Grain

The direction in which the grain of wood runs can be determined by observing the markings on the surface. If the cut is made parallel to the streaks in the wood, it has been sawed with the grain. Cutting across them is sawing against the grain.

It is important whether one saws with or against the grain for two reasons—appearance and strength. From the standpoint of appearance, the grain should always run with the length of a piece, against its width.

The streaks in the wood of the top of a chest of drawers, for instance, should run from left to right when viewed from the front. On the side they should run from top to bottom. In the same way, the grain of a table top should run parallel to its longer side, and of the legs from top to bottom.

In pieces of the size mentioned, strength is of no consideration, but in small, fragile pieces, it is extremely important. A very narrow strip, particularly if the wood is thin, will break easily if cut against the grain.

When making a miniature copy of a full-sized piece of furniture, the craftsman will sometimes cut a section in one piece that in the full-sized model, mostly for reasons of economy, was composed of several sections joined together. The miniature section, if it is shaped in curves or angles, must often run both with and against the grain. This cannot be helped and is not important if the pieces are fairly wide (possibly $\frac{3}{16}$ inch or so), or if the wood is at least $\frac{1}{16}$ inch thick. If not, extra care must be given during the sanding and finishing processes so that the parts cut against the grain do not break.

The same is true of a frame that is cut in one piece. If the frame's sides are very narrow, the longer sides which were cut with the grain will cause no problem, but the shorter sides must be handled carefully. If, during sanding, one of the shorter sides should snap, the break is usually a clean one and can be glued so as to be invisible.

Except for special designs such as those used in inlay work, the grain should always run lengthwise or up and down, never on the diagonal.

Sawing Along One Edge of a Line

In making full-size furniture, straight cuts are made with a circular saw which is equipped with a fence against which the wood is pressed as it is being cut. In this way, the cut edges are perfectly straight and true.

Wood must be fed through a jigsaw without such a guide, however, and as expert as the operator may be, there are bound to be slight imperfections in straight cuts. Although these imperfections may not be visible to the eye and do not usually affect furniture quality, they are important when the edges of two pieces of wood are to be glued together at an angle. If the edges are held together in the position in which they are to be glued and the line of contact held to the light, the spots at which the two pieces do not touch can easily be seen.

Filing the imperfect edges will bring them quickly into alignment so that they can be glued together perfectly. There is no way, however, to replace wood that has been sawed away. For this reason, it is best when cutting pieces that are to be fitted together to saw along the outside edge of a drawn line rather than straight down the line's center. This method will ensure a tiny amount of excess wood which will allow for later filing to make a perfectly straight edge.

This procedure is of particular importance in constructing a piece that will nest inside another piece, or in cutting a frame for a mirror. It is virtually impossible to saw a frame so perfectly that it will fit snugly all around a mirror. By following the outside of a drawn line, the craftsman can leave a little extra wood around the opening. He can then file, measure, and file again, until a perfect fit has been attained.

A little extra wood should also be left at the ends of pieces whose exact length is important. Rungs and splats of a chair, for instance, should be cut a fraction of an inch longer than their patterns and later sanded to an exact fit.

Mitering

Mitering is the joining of two edges which have been cut on 45-degree angles so that the only visible part of the joint is a thin line at the corner. In good cabinetwork, it is necessary that all corners be mitered if they will show in the finished piece. This includes the joining of the ends of narrow strips as well as the sides of larger pieces. If a corner were not mitered, the edge of one of the pieces would be exposed and the joint would be unattractive. Mitered and unmitered corners are shown in the illustration.

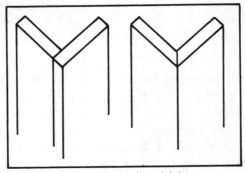

Unmitered and mitered joints.

To "bevel" an edge is to cut it on an angle, and two beveled edges are needed for a mitered joint. If the saw has a table that can be tilted, beveling edges is a simple operation. The thumbscrew that holds the table in position is loosened, and the table is tilted until the arrow (usually located under the table close to the thumbscrew) indicates that the slant is 45 degrees. The screw is then tightened to hold the table in that position.

In sawing a beveled edge, there are three important points to note:

Cutting a beveled edge on tilted saw table.

1.   The drawn line to be followed must be on the outside of the wood—on the surface that will show in the finished piece.

2.   Care must be taken to make sure that the sawed bevel will slant in the right direction. Whether the saw's table is tilted to the right or left will affect the slant of the cut. The slant will also be affected by the edge the operator chooses to enter to start sawing.

It is therefore necessary that the cut be visualized before it is made. Holding the wood on the tilted table close to the blade and picturing at what angle the blade will cut is a help in this procedure. Only after the operator is sure that the bevel will be slanted correctly should the sawing start.

3.   For square-cut edges, the saw's table is level, the pressure of the blade against the wood is in an up-and-down direction. It is only necessary, then, to press the wood down in order to keep it from slipping. However, when the table is tilted, the blade has a tendency to push the wood down sideways, in the direction of the tilt.

Extra care must therefore be taken to hold the work steady as it is being sawed. Not only should it be pressed flat against the table, it should also be pressed slightly upward, toward the blade, while being cut.

Another method of holding the wood in position while beveling an edge is to clamp a straight-edge piece of wood to the table to be used as a guide. In this case, however, the wood being cut must have perfectly parallel sides, and if the piece is very small, it is more practicable to guide it by hand.

Whichever method is used, it should be practiced a few times on scrap wood before it is used to cut a pattern.

An edge that has been sawed at a right angle may be filed and sanded as much as necessary. One must be more careful, however, with a beveled cut. Its edge is very thin and can too easily be sanded off. If any straightening of the edges is necessary, the sanding should be done lightly. Later, when the two beveled edges have been glued together in a mitered joint, the corner can be sanded more heavily to smooth it.

If the saw does not have a table that can be tilted, a mitering box (usually available in hobby shops) can be used. The mitering box holds the wood in a vertical position, at the proper angle, and the beveled edge is then cut with a hand saw.

Sawing Identical Pieces

There are occasions when two or more cut pieces must be identical. If matching pieces on a piece of furniture are to be separated by a slight distance, such as the two arms of a sofa, a small difference between them will not be noticed. However, if they are to be used close together, they should be exactly the same. For instance, even a small alteration in the curve of one leg of a pedestal table can mar the appearance of the whole table.

The method described here of sawing identical pieces is a timesaving and simple operation. Assuming four legs for a table are needed, only one pattern is drawn. Four pieces of wood a little larger than the pattern are then cut, spread with rubber cement and stacked evenly. The pattern is cemented on the top piece. The stack is then pressed together with clamps or spring clips and set aside to dry for a half hour or so.

The pieces are then cut as one, following the pattern, after which they are separated and the wood rubbed clean of rubber cement with the fingers. (When separating very narrow or fragile pieces, it is best to slide them apart sideways, as one would open a fan. Pulling a delicate piece upward could cause it to break.)

If the wood to be used is so thick that the saw cannot cut easily through the required number of layers, the pieces must be cut either separately or in two stacks. In this case the patterns at least should be identical. (The method for drawing identical patterns is discussed in chapter 4.)

Cutting Very Small Pieces

If he is wise, the maker of miniature furniture will make use of even the smallest scrap of leftover wood. This is particularly true if the scrap happens to be a piece of scarce and valuable wood such as rosewood, teak, or mahogany. A piece an inch square might very well end up as the arm of a chair or the face of a drawer. It is necessary, then, that he learn how to handle it.

Cutting very small pieces presents a special problem because of the hole in the saw's table. When the table of the saw is level, the opening through which the blade passes need not be much larger than the width of the blade itself. However, the table of a good jigsaw is made so that it can be tilted for making beveled cuts, and when the table is tilted, the opening needs to be an inch or so wide to accommodate the blade. Any jigsaw the craftsman is likely to buy will have a table with the wider opening in it.

To saw a very small piece of wood when the opening beneath it is almost as large as (and in some cases larger than) the wood itself can be a nuisance. For one thing, the wood being cut does not have enough support. For another, the piece is apt to drop through the opening and disappear into the lower regions of the saw as soon as it is cut.

The solution to the problem is simple. One need only lay the small piece of wood on a larger one, near the edge, and cut the two together. The smaller piece must be pressed down tightly

against the other while the sawing is in progress to prevent slipping.

It is not necessary that the supporting piece be manipulated
along with the small one during the cutting. It can be held
firmly with one hand and the top piece turned with the fingers
of the other hand and cut as desired.

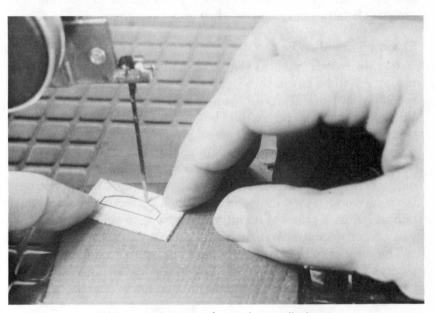

Using wood support for sawing small piece.

The supporting piece may be of any inexpensive, soft wood
and of a size that can be handled easily—perhaps four or five
inches across and $\frac{1}{16}$ inch thick. It can be saved for this one purpose and used over and over.

A word of warning about the handling of tiny sawed pieces
should be added here. Although it has not yet been explained
scientifically, it is a fact (witnessed many times by the writer)
that minute, unattached pieces have a life of their own. They
crawl over the edges of workbenches and drop into limbo; they
hide in wastebaskets and in the pile of carpets; they drop from
the fingers and, under the very eyes of the craftsman, disappear

instantaneously from the exact spot onto which they fell.

It is also a frustrating fact that while a few of these elusive pieces do turn up later, they do so only after duplicates have been cut and the furniture for which they were intended long since finished.

It is imperative, therefore, that a small box be kept beside the saw and that all small pieces be dropped into it as soon as they are cut. It is the only way to trap and keep them.

Sawing Thin Wood

Very thin woods, such as veneer or $\frac{1}{32}$-inch plywood, especially if they are to be cut in thin strips or intricate patterns, present a special problem. The vibration of the blade against a wider, thicker piece causes no trouble, but when very thin wood is used, protruding parts of a shaped piece may break off during sawing, or extremely thin strips may snap in half.

In addition, if thin plywood is being used, the vibration of the blade can knock off small chips along the edges of the bottom layer of wood. Since the edge of $\frac{1}{32}$-inch plywood is usually left uncovered in a piece of furniture, the gaps in the bottom layer will be conspicuous, and the piece cannot be used.

The answer to the problem is the same as that in the preceding section on cutting small pieces. The thin wood is easily cut if it is laid on another, thicker piece and the two sawed together. There

Cutting thin wood on plywood support.

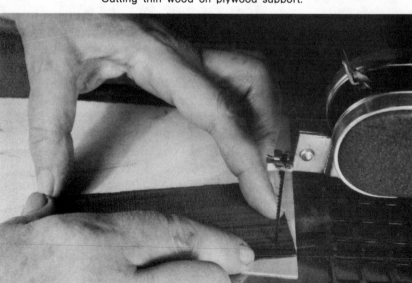

will then be no breaking or splintering of the piece on top.

(Incidentally, if a piece of veneer with straight sides is needed, it can usually be cut successfully with an ordinary pair of scissors.)

Making Cabriole Legs

Whether or not the craftsman is a student of furniture styles, and even though he may not know the name, the gracefully curved shape of the cabriole leg is familiar to everyone. It was much used in early French furniture, in Queen Anne furniture—so much so that the same shape is also known as the "Queen Anne leg"—and is still widely used today.

It is important that the craftsman who takes miniature furniture seriously learn how to make the cabriole leg. No special skill is required, but the method should be understood and a little practice may be needed.

In principle, the cabriole leg is made of a piece of wood shaped on all four sides instead of the usual two. If the necessary cuts were to be made separately and the excess wood discarded after each cut, the piece would gradually become so irregularly shaped that it could not be held firmly enough to make the final cuts.

Using the method described here, however, all the work is done on a square piece of wood whose four flat sides are not disturbed at all during the necessary operations. In this way the piece is easy to handle and to saw accurately all the way through the fifth and final cut.

First, two identical patterns are drawn for each leg wanted, the second pattern in reverse so that the drawn legs are facing each other. The patterns are then cut from the sheet of paper in rectangles with approximately ⅛-inch margins left at the sides and bottoms of the legs, as shown in Figure 1. No margins are left at the tops.

Next, a square stick of wood is needed, with sides as wide as the pattern. It will not matter if the wood is a little wider than necessary but it must not be less than the width of the drawn legs plus the margins. The length of the wood piece is not important; it should be long enough to be handled easily and perhaps long enough so that more legs can be cut from it later on.

The patterns are then attached with rubber cement to the wood on two adjacent sides as shown in Figure 2. The legs should face each other and the tops of the patterns be flush with the top edges of the wood.

**MAKING A
CABRIOLE
LEG**

Figure 1

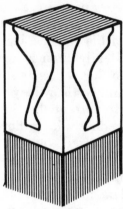

Figure 2

The piece is now ready to cut. If the blade in the saw has had considerable use, it would be well to put in a fresh one at this point. This will make it easier to cut pattern lines accurately in wood that is abnormally thick.

The first four cuts are shown in Figure 3. The lines of the legs are sawed from the tops to about ⅛ inch below the feet. The wood is withdrawn after each cut and the next one started at the

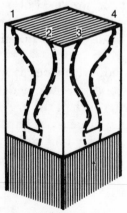

Figure 3

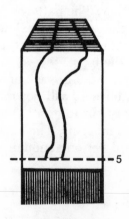

Figure 4

top. Since the whole purpose of this method is to keep the wood in one piece, the blade should not saw through the sides or bottom of the wood piece until the final cut.

The fifth and last cut is shown in Figure 4. With the sawed end of the wood held firmly together in the fingers, the piece is cut straight across at the bottom of the foot.

The cut end of the wood, still held together with the fingers, is now dropped into the palm of the other hand, and a miracle occurs. Nine pieces of wood fall apart, each one looking very much like a distorted cabriole leg. Upon closer examination, however, the one in the center is perfect. A special satisfaction is in store for the craftsman who has yet to make his first cabriole leg.

This method of sawing is useful not only for cabriole legs, but for any piece that's to be shaped on four sides. Tapered legs, for example, are easily cut in this way. If the leg is tapered on the sides only, it is cut in the usual way from a flat piece of wood. However, if the front and back are also tapered, two matching patterns are drawn, and the method described above is followed.

Pieces which are not symmetrical may also be cut by this method, but the two patterns will not be the same. A sofa, for instance, with cabriole legs at the front corners, will often have a third leg in the center which is shaped differently so that it will fit the straight line of the front. Suggested patterns for this center leg are shown in the accompanying illustration.

For center leg, patterns do not match.

The arm of a chair which curves outward when viewed from above and dips down when viewed from the side may also be cut from two patterns which do not match.

This method of shaping four sides at once is so adaptable that the craftsman should experiment with it. He can originate his own patterns as needs arise, first trying them out on scrap wood.

6

Using Other Tools

Although it will be helpful for the craftsman to know in advance as much as possible about the tools he is learning to use, practice is by far the best teacher. Operations that at first seem awkward to do can soon be done so automatically that it will be possible to concentrate on the work being done rather than on the mechanics of doing it. It is at this point that the real pleasure of using any tool begins.

The jigsaw has already been covered in the previous chapter. Other tools the craftsman may wish to use will be discussed in the following pages.

Variable-Speed Drill

Although a hand drill is often held in both hands when used for larger work, for miniature work it is best to hold it as one would hold a pencil, with the fingers close to the turning bit. The other hand is then left free to hold the workpiece.

There are no rules as to which speeds to use, and the craftsman will soon learn which are best for the job he is doing. The slowest speed will allow for the greatest accuracy and control, but a faster speed will be necessary when a fairly large bit is being used to drill into hardwood. The best advice to be given is that a slow speed should be used at first and can be increased when necessary.

Similarly, the amount of pressure that should be exerted against the drill follows no rules. When drilling small holes, the bit itself does most of the work and very little pressure is needed. For carving with rounded bits on hardwood, the craftsman will probably find that the pressure should be increased.

Drilling Holes

Before drilling a hole, it is always necessary to mark with a sharp pencil point the exact spot where the hole is to be. A small, shallow indentation is then made in the wood on the spot. The point of a safety pin, or any sharp, pointed instrument can be used for this purpose. The dent will prevent the turning bit from

DRILLING A HOLE

Marking location with pencil.

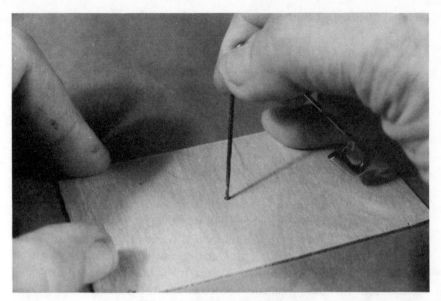

Making indention with safety pin.

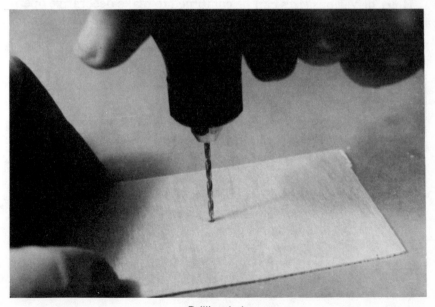

Drilling hole.

slipping sideways on the surface until it has had a chance to start cutting into the wood.

To make sure the hole to be drilled will be the right size for the pin or tack that will go into it, the bit should first be tried out on a scrap of wood. Pressure should have to be applied to push the pin into the hole; if it slips in easily, the next smaller-size bit should be used.

The angle at which the drill is held is important. Unless a slanting hole is needed, the drill should be held at an exact right angle to the wood. Using the slowest speed, the hole is then started, after which the speed can be increased.

Until the craftsman has gained experience, he should always keep in mind that an electric drill works very quickly. If a hole is to go only halfway through a piece of wood, the drilling must be done cautiously. There is nothing more disconcerting than to find that a hole which was meant for a leg in the bottom of a chair seat has also become a hole in the top surface.

Decorative Holes

Holes of various sizes can be combined to make decorative openings, where appropriate, in the railings of spindle-back chairs,

Drilled holes in splat of Windsor chair.

cabinet doors and the like. In most cases, the same designs can be cut with a jigsaw. However, if the patterns lend themselves to a combination of round holes, a hand drill will do the job more quickly and accurately. The illustrations show some of the designs that can be cut in this way. The heart-shaped openings, a motif popular in the eighteenth and early nineteenth centuries, can be made by drilling three overlapping holes, as illustrated, then by filing or sawing away the shaded areas.

Decorative holes can be made with a hand drill.

The drill can also be used instead of the saw for making round, inside cuts along the edge of a chair rail, or other similar pieces, as shown. The small branchlike decorations on the doors of the wardrobe (shown in the following section on carving) were made by using the drill for the round cuts along the edges.

Since it is necessary that decorative holes be positioned accurately, it is usually safer to drill them before the paper pattern is glued to the wood (for later sawing). That part of the pattern which would conceal the drilled holes is cut away so that they can be seen. The pattern can then be positioned correctly, glued into place, and the outline of the piece sawed to shape.

Sanding with a Drill
Small sanding discs which fit in the drill are sometimes useful for

comparatively large areas of miniature work and save time when a sizable amount of wood is to be removed from the edges. The craftsman will probably find, however, that most sanding jobs on miniature pieces can more easily be controlled if done by hand.

Carving

Making miniature carvings with a hand drill is fascinating work. Although a pattern for the design should first be drawn on paper, it should be used only as a visual guide. It is necessary that the work be seen as it progresses, and a pattern glued to the wood would make this impossible.

General design for carved medallion.

Since plans for an intricate carving will change as the work goes along, only a general design should be drawn on paper. More often than not, one cut will suggest the next one and (as the accompanying illustrations show) the finished work will probably only vaguely resemble the original drawing. The reason for this is that cuts made by drill bits are wider than pencil lines, and it would be very difficult to make a detailed drawing that would allow for the various bits that will be used, or for the angle at which the drill will be held for each cut.

Since a paper pattern cannot be glued to the wood, it would seem logical that the entire pattern could be drawn on the wood itself, but this is not practicable. Before the work progresses very far, some of the lines would disappear under sawdust or be otherwise erased, because nearby cuts will be wider than the pattern lines. It is therefore better to draw only a few lines at a time on the wood, to cut these, then to draw and cut the next few. Using a fine bit that will make as thin a line as possible, the whole design is outlined in this way, as shown in the illustration, before any finished carving is done.

Whether it is better to follow a line in a steady progression or to move the drill back and forth with a sketching motion is for the craftsman to decide. Some woods have tiny, invisible hard spots which tend to push the bit off its course. The sketching motion is a better choice here as it minimizes the danger of this happening.

The piece being carved must be pressed firmly against a flat surface. Without support from beneath, the pressure and vibration of the drill would make it impossible to hold the wood steady. Pieces too small to be kept in position with the fingers can be fastened with rubber cement to a larger piece of wood. If the cement does not hold well enough, white glue may be used. While this will make separating the small piece from the larger one more difficult, it can be done easily enough by using a sharp-edged instrument like a razor blade.

CARVING A MEDALLION

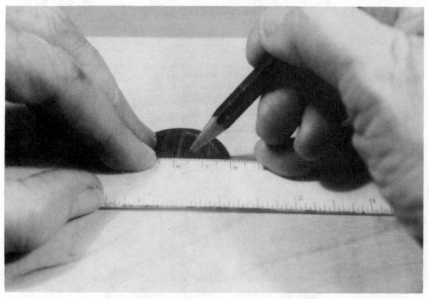

First lines of pattern are drawn on wood.

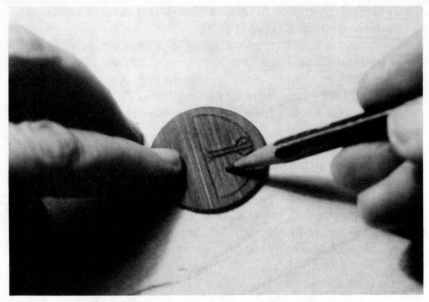

Drawn lines have been cut and drawing continues.

Outlining of pattern almost completed.

Cuts have been deepened and background routed out.

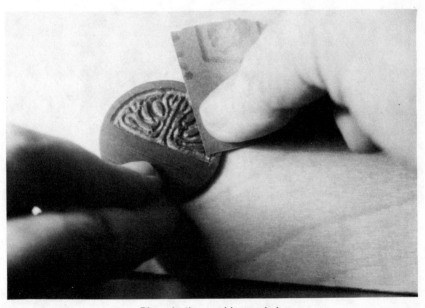

Piece is thoroughly sanded.

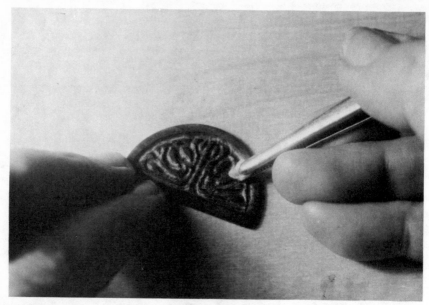

Dust is removed with tack cloth.

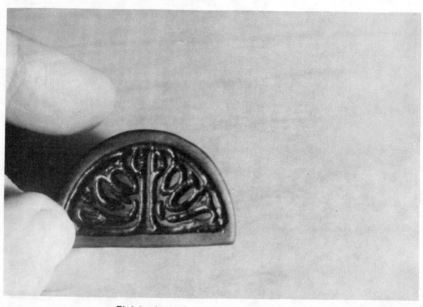

Finished carving, waxed and polished.

This method of fastening small bits of wood to a larger piece makes possible the carving of trim as small as ⅛ inch across. The patterns of such pieces must, of course, be simple, but carvings on comparatively small areas of full-sized furniture are usually the same. On such pieces in miniature, the lines of a shell, or the petals and center of a flower, are all that are necessary.

For easier carving, tiny shell is temporarily glued to larger wood piece.

After the entire pattern has been outlined as described above, the design is then deepened and embellished with whatever bits the craftsman wishes to use. Short of allowing a bit to go all the way through the wood, a carving can hardly be cut too deep. Among other things, a full-size carving is judged by the depth at which it is cut, and a miniature carving is no different. A design scratched in the wood's surface is not a carving; cuts should be deepened until the pattern, when held at an angle to the light, throws rich shadows.

Carvings may be either simple, deeply cut line drawings, or they may be done in relief. To make a relief carving, the pattern is first outlined with a fine bit as described above, after which the background is routed away with the use of a router bit, or a small, cylindrical- or ball-shaped bit. If the edges of the remaining raised design are sharp and angled, they should then be rounded off with sandpaper.

Carvings on furniture are handled in one of two ways—they are either cut on the wood of the furniture itself, or on separate pieces which are then glued to the wood. Since a separate piece is easier to handle, and a whole furniture part is not spoiled if the carving is not successful, the latter method is preferable. It is not often a matter of choice, however, and a study of the model will show whether or not the carving can be done separately.

In many full-size carvings there are small, shaped, open spaces which go all the way through the wood. In miniature work, some of these areas are so small that to cut many of them with a saw would be time-consuming and tedious work. The writer has tried a method which works very well, and the craftsman may wish to use it.

The first illustration shows a way of cutting the open areas around a carved inset. The pattern is first drawn on graph paper, then glued to the wood and the circle sawed out. The cut must be made in one continuous line, as illustrated, so that when the leaf is glued back into place, it will fit perfectly.

The open spaces around the leaf, shaded in the illustration, are then removed with a jigsaw. The paper pattern can next be removed, the leaf carved with a drill, and its edges rounded off and smoothed by sanding. When sanding, care should be taken to leave untouched those areas that will come into contact with the frame when the leaf is glued back into place. Similar care should be taken when sanding the frame itself. Although its surface edges may be rounded off as much as desired, sanding of the inner circle must be done so lightly that it will not be even slightly enlarged, nor its shape changed.

The furniture piece is then sawed to shape after which the leaf is glued back into its frame. Very seldom are there any noticeable cracks in the joints between the leaf tips and the frame, but if there are, they should be filled with wood filler. The final step is to sand the joints until they are invisible.

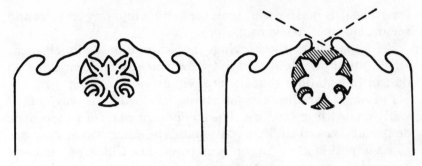

A difficult carving simplified.

The next illustration shows a section of a more complicated carving. As with the leaf inset above, the paper pattern is fastened to the wood, but this time the outline of the furniture piece is cut first. The section to be carved is then separated from the body of the piece along the dotted line shown. In order that the three open spaces in the carving can be reached with a saw, three cuts along the outer edge of the carving are made as shown. All the unwanted wood, shaded in the illustration, can now be sawed away. The paper pattern is next removed, the necessary carving is done, and the carved pieces reassembled and glued back into place. If the work is done carefully, the strategically located joints will not be seen.

Dividing an elaborate carving into sections.

Although thorough sanding of miniature carvings is rather tedious work, the more that can be done, the better. Small files, the edges of folded sandpaper, and short, narrow strips cut from emery boards make useful tools for getting into tiny crevices and smoothing small background areas.

Before staining, the carvings should be thoroughly cleaned. Small bits of tackcloth held in tweezers are useful for picking up dust in indentations that surface wiping cannot reach.

Full-sized carvings are sometimes handled in a way that is easily copied in miniature. The component parts of a picture or design are sawed and carved separately, after which they are glued in position to a background piece. The Chinese screen and doors of the wardrobe shown here were decorated in this way.

Screen decorated with cut-out, glued-on pieces.

Lathe Work

Even on his first try, the craftsman will probably make a successful turned piece. The skill needed for such work is not in making a piece attractive, but in making one that follows a planned pattern, or in making two that match. For his first try, therefore, it would be wise for the craftsman to turn a piece whose exact pattern is not important, and one that can be used singly, such as a lamp base, or the pedestal for a table.

The wood used may be either a length cut from a ready-made dowel, or a piece made by sawing a square stick of wood, fasten-

Wardrobe decorated with cut-out, glued-on pieces.

ing it in the lathe, and rounding it as it turns. Both the ready-made dowel and the one which has been rounded on the lathe by the craftsman have advantages and disadvantages.

The advantage of the former is that a ready-made dowel can be bought in any wanted diameter and for use need only be cut into short lengths. Its disadvantages are two: the light color of the wood will probably not match the wood used for the rest of the furniture piece, and it is sometimes difficult to stain it to the exact color wanted. Also, it is hard to fasten the end of a length of wood to a rounded surface. When some styles of furniture require such joints to be made, it is necessary to leave flat areas at those points on a turned piece. For example, such flat areas may be required on a turned chair leg where the seat and stretchers are to be attached, as illustrated. If the leg has been made from a round dowel, these joint areas must be squared off by hand, with the use of either a small hand saw or a file.

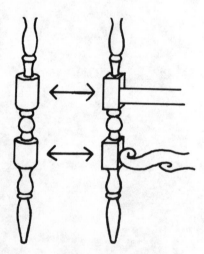

Chair leg is usually squared off where it joins seat and stretcher.

The only two disadvantages in making a dowel from a square stick are, first, the time and work involved and, second, the difficulty of centering a square piece in most chucks. The advantages of such a dowel are that it can be made of the same wood used for the rest of the furniture piece, which eliminates the problem of finishing woods of different grains and colors, and, since it is already square, the areas where joints are to be made can simply be left as they are when the rest of the piece is rounded off.

(Some styles of chairs, such as a Windsor chair, have thin stretchers which are inserted into holes drilled in the legs, as shown. In such cases, no flat areas need be left in the legs when they are shaped.)

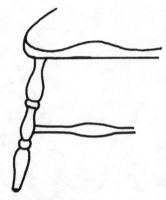

With some chair styles, thin stretcher can be inserted into hole drilled in leg.

To allow for wood that will be cut away during turning, the dowel used must be slightly larger in diameter than the pattern. It should be no longer than necessary (an inch longer than the pattern is enough) since unnecessary length may cause a thin dowel to curve under pressure as it is being turned.

As mentioned in chapter 2, the workpiece must be exactly centered in the lathe, so that it will not wobble as it turns. Any one of the chucks listed, except the 4-jaw chuck, automatically centers the left end of the workpiece, but if any other accessory is used, the left end must be centered by the craftsman himself. In any case, the right end of the workpiece must always be centered by hand; there is no accessory which does this automatically.

To center a dowel, the same procedure is followed that was described for drilling a hole. The exact center on the end (or both ends) of the dowel is marked with a pencil and an indentation made into which the point of the lathe center will go.

The left end of the dowel is then mounted in the left end of the lathe, following the manufacturer's instructions for whichever accessory is being used. Next, the lathe's adjustable right end is moved inward until the point of its lathe center fits snugly into the indentation in the right end of the dowel, as illustrated, and is secured in this position.

Centering dowel in right end of lathe.

Before work is begun, the pattern to be turned is first drawn on graph paper. The length of each section in the pattern is then measured, and the dowel marked with heavy pencil lines in corresponding sections, as shown. These lines do not need to circle the dowel; as it turns in the lathe, the marks will show as continuous lines. Using this method of dividing the dowel into sections, the craftsman will be able not only to follow a pattern, but to make as many matching pieces as needed.

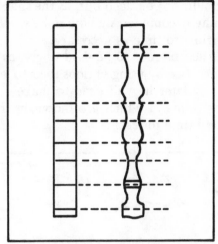

Marking dowel to follow sections in pattern.

The marked dowel is then mounted in the lathe as described above, and the work of shaping can begin. First, the pencil lines —which would soon disappear as the work progresses—are cut into the wood with a sharp-edged tool. The cutting tool is held above each pencil line, as illustrated, and pressed gently against the dowel until the cut is clearly visible.

Cutting marked lines into dowel with sharp-edged tool.

These cuts should not be deep but, as the shaping progresses, some of them may become too shallow to be seen and should be deepened from time to time as necessary.

If the first turned piece is to be used singly, as suggested, the craftsman can practice by using various tools to learn what each will do. Sooner or later he will need to make a variety of the standard shapes, some of which are shown in the illustration, and this is a good time to learn.

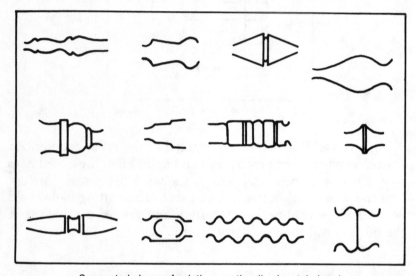

Suggested shapes for lathe practice (horizontal views).

The shaping tools (narrow, shaped files work best for miniature work) should be held against the wood without heavy pressure. This is particularly important when, after the shaping is almost finished, there may be thin areas in the workpiece. These can snap under too much pressure and, although such breaks can often be mended with epoxy and a tiny dowel, it is best to be careful to avoid such an accident.

The craftsman will find that a sharp-edged file will be one of the shaping tools he uses most. Not only will it cut the marked lines described above, but also, if the cutting edge is left in one of the grooves as the workpiece turns, and the tool tilted gently to

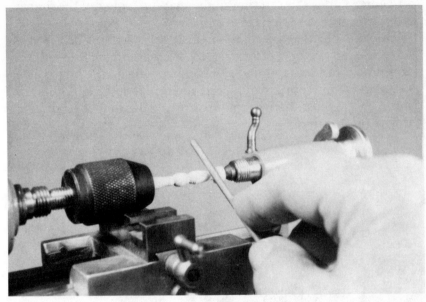

Narrow files make useful shaping tools.

the left and right, the edges of the cut can be rounded off as much as desired. There is no need for each shape to have a special tool. Many of the shapes shown can be made with just a sharp-edged flat file and a round one.

When the shaping is finished, the workpiece can be removed from the lathe and the unwanted ends sawed off. There is an alternative method of removing it, however, that will leave one end with a small knob that can be used as the top of a post, finial, or urn. The sharp-edged file is simply used to cut all the way through the workpiece as it turns in the lathe. When the workpiece snaps at the point being cut, it will drop from the lathe. The end without the knob is then sawed off flat.

Using the Hand Drill as a Lathe
If a turned piece is wanted that is too thin and short to shape on a lathe, a hand drill can be used. The writer has found this method works very well if the workpiece is no more than about ¾ inch in length. If it is too long, the unsupported end will turn

off-center under the pressure of the shaping tool, and the shaped piece will not be symmetrical.

The short dowel piece is inserted in the hand-drill chuck where the bit would normally go. With the chuck tightened, the drill is held in one hand and a very narrow file in the other, as illustrated. A moderate drill speed should be used, and pressure of the tool against the workpiece as it is being shaped, should be as light as possible.

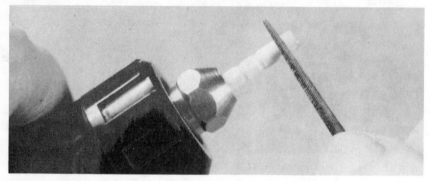

For very small turnings, hand drill can be used as lathe.

The small posts between the shelves of the étagère shown **in the next illustration** were shaped in a hand drill.

Using a Circular Saw

Care should be taken when using a circular saw, a tool not quite as harmless as the jigsaw. The hand holding the wood should never be positioned in line with the blade. In addition, the guard should be kept over the blade at all times except when a beveled edge is being cut. In such a case, the blade is tilted and the guard will not fit over it.

Depending upon which type of cut is being made, one of two attachments is used to guide the wood. For a "rip cut" (a cut along the length of a wood piece) the rip fence is used. The fence should be clamped to the table so that it is exactly parallel to the blade.

When making a "cross cut" (a cut across the width of the

Posts between shelves of étagère were turned in hand drill.

wood), or when mitering an edge, the miter gauge is used. The miter gauge fits into either of two slots on the saw's table, and is used to push the wood forward during a sawing operation. The manufacturer's instructions should be followed when setting up either attachment for use.

The circular blade can be raised or lowered according to the thickness of the wood being cut. The higher the blade is set, the less strain there will be on the motor, but a blade that is set higher than necessary is more dangerous to use. It is therefore best to set the blade so that it barely protrudes above the wood surface as it cuts. If the motor starts to labor after the saw has been used for a while, the blade can then be raised a little. The better the saw's quality, the less chance there will be that the motor will slow down or become overheated.

Since a circular saw blade takes a fairly wide bite out of the wood as it cuts, it is important that the rip fence be attached with great accuracy. The blade should not enter the wood in the middle of a pattern line, but at its outside edge so that the cut piece will be of the full wanted width. If two matching narrow strips are wanted, it is better not to try to cut one wider piece exactly in half, because the thickness of the blade would then have to be taken into consideration, a difficult thing to do. Instead, each strip should be cut separately from a wider piece of wood. In this way, the blade can be positioned at the edge of each pattern line as mentioned above.

Soldering

There are two kinds of solder the craftsman can use—hard or

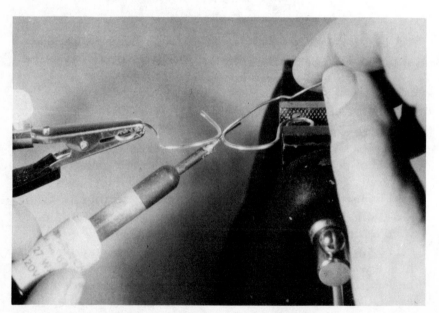

Hot soldering iron is held under and touching metal pieces to be joined.

soft. Soft solder is made of tin and lead and has a lower melting point than hard solder. It is therefore easier to use. Hard, or silver, solder makes a stronger joint. Since there is no need for extra strength in miniature metal furniture, soft solder is recommended.

Soldering small metal pieces is delicate, but not difficult, work. The ideal soldered joint is strong but has been made with the least possible amount of solder. It is this last condition that will require some practice. However, fortunately for the beginner, soft solder is easily filed and flattened, so if the first joints he makes are large and unsightly, they can be made less conspicuous with a little careful filing. The joint can then be pointed to match the metal being used.

The metal pieces to be soldered must first be thoroughly cleaned with a material called "flux." Flux may either be bought separately, or soldering wire is available with a hollow core in which the flux is enclosed. In this form, the flux is released onto the metal as the work is being done. For miniature work, solder with flux in its core is by far the more convenient to use.

With two exceptions, soft solder will join any metals the craftsman is likely to use. The exceptions are aluminum, which requires a special solder, and lead. Lead has such a low melting point that a hot iron would melt it as quickly as the solder itself.

Although soft solder melts easily, it solidifies almost instantly

Dollhouse bed was used as base for making brass bed shown in foreground.

once the source of heat has been removed. If the melted solder is dropped onto cold metal, it will solidify before it has had time to complete the joint. To make a strong joint, therefore, the metal must also be heated.

If the iron were applied directly to the solder, an unnecessarily large amount of it might melt and be released onto the metal pieces. The resulting joint would be unsightly. In order to avoid this, and to heat the metal at the same time, it is best to hold the hot iron under and touching the metal pieces at the point where they are to be joined, and to let the hot metal, not the iron itself, melt the solder. The end of the soldering wire is held against the joint, on top, as illustrated. As soon as the hot metal melts the solder to the point that a small amount of it is released onto the joint, both the soldering wire and iron are moved away, and if all has gone well, the joint is completed.

The tip of the soldering iron should always be kept clean of solder that is apt to accumulate on it. The purchase of special products made for this purpose is unnecessary. Wiping the hot iron on a wet cloth from time to time will remove small amounts of excess solder, and if a large amount has accumulated, it can easily be filed away (while the iron is cold) until the original tip is exposed.

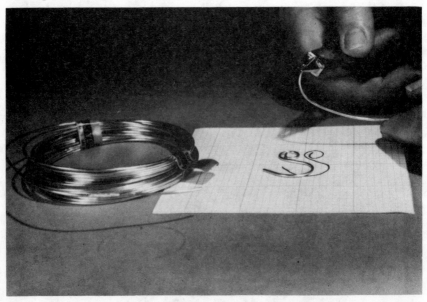

Using a pattern to aid bending matched wire pieces.

Shaped wires make grill for windup phonograph.

During a soldering operation there are four objects to be held —the iron, the solder, and the two metal pieces to be joined— but the craftsman has only two hands. Since the iron and solder need to be hand-held in order to be manipulated as needed, the metal pieces must be supported in some way with the points to be joined touching. Two small vises can be used for this purpose, or a single vise with two opposing clamps (pictured in chapter 2) made especially for small soldering jobs. The metal pieces may also be supported between heavy blocks of wood or metal. Any method at all can be used that will hold them firmly in position.

Since the craftsman has only wire, metal sheets and bits of jewelry or other shaped pieces with which to work, the variety of

metal furniture he can make at home is limited. Factory
machines such as die-casting equipment and machining tools are
needed for specially shaped pieces. He can, however, buy metal
dollhouse furniture and modify it in any way he chooses.

The two beds shown in the illustration are an example. The
bed on the left is widely sold as a child's bed for a dollhouse. Its
width was correct for the writer's scale, but it was too short. The
frame was therefore cut in half and connecting pieces soldered
on either side to lengthen it.

Two rods from both the head and foot were removed to make
room for the curved wires. Lengths of brass wire were then
shaped as shown and soldered into place. Using Polyform, the
leaves were formed right onto the wires and hardened by baking
the whole bed in a slow oven. The leaves were then painted with
brass metallic paint.

Bending Wire

For bending wire, a pair of needlenose pliers whose jaws taper to
a point is the easiest tool to use. Such pliers sometimes have one
square jaw for bending angles and one round jaw for bending
curves. With others, the jaws are both either round or square.

When lengths of wire are to be shaped for making brass or
iron furniture, it is usually necessary to bend the pieces in matching pairs so that the left side of the pattern will match the
right. In order to do this, the wanted curves are drawn on paper
and the drawing used as a guide during the wire-bending process.
The wire piece is checked against the pattern from time to time,
as illustrated. In this way, it is not difficult to make as many
matching pieces as needed.

When bending wire, the first instinct is to grasp the wire
firmly in the pliers' jaws and to give the tool a vigorous twist.
This method, however, tends to pull out of shape the curves that
have already been made. The best way to curve wire is to grasp
it every $\frac{1}{16}$ inch or so with the pliers and to bend it only slightly
each time. The curve is then deepened by repeating the procedure until the desired shape has been reached, after which
the excess wire is trimmed from the ends with a wire-cutting
tool.

7

Adhesives

Although some of today's adhesives can almost work miracles, not even the best of them are satisfactory when used under the wrong conditions. The material to be glued should be clean, dry, and free of grease or oil. In addition, all adhesives work better if pressure is applied during the drying or setting periods.

When making miniature furniture, the requirement of clean material presents a problem to which there is no clear-cut solution. It is easier to stain and finish small pieces of wood before they are glued together, in which case the adhesive used cannot work at its best. On the other hand, if the stain is applied after the adhesive, and traces of excess adhesive are left around a joint, the stain will not be able to penetrate the wood in that area. The result will be a permanent, light-colored line around the joint.

Another consideration is that if there are hard-to-reach places on the furniture, such as the backs of spindles and the grooves in carving, it is difficult to finish the wood after assembly.

Whether it is better to glue or to finish first depends upon the individual piece, so the choice is up to the craftsman. It would

Different adhesives have special uses.

seem that a compromise is the best answer. The main body of the piece can be glued, then finished. The small, intricate parts, which will probably not receive the brunt of any future mishandling, can be finished first, then glued into place.

If finishing is done first, the adhesive used can be given a chance to do its best if the surfaces to be glued are roughened with a pinpoint or sharp, pointed instrument until some of the raw wood is exposed. If such surfaces are large enough, they can be sanded clean or protected during finishing with masking tape. Anything that will allow the adhesive to reach clean wood will be helpful.

An adhesive should be applied thinly and not all the way to the edges. Under pressure, it will be forced to the edges and, hopefully, no farther. If it does squeeze out beyond the joint, the excess should be removed immediately. A thin adhesive can be wiped off with a cloth. One with more body can be removed by using the point of a toothpick. Whatever method is used, the work should be done as quickly as possible, before the adhesive dries.

Whenever two flat pieces are being glued, they should either be weighted down or clamped together during the drying or setting period recommended by the manufacturer of the particular adhesive.

There will be many times, however, when clamps cannot be used and small, irregularly shaped pieces must be pressed together and held with the fingers. Since such a position cannot be held long enough for most adhesives to dry completely, pressing with the fingers is not an ideal method for obtaining a fast bond. However, when there is no other choice, the bond is usually a satisfactory one if, in future years, undue strain is not put on the pieces glued in this way.

At the very least, the craftsman will need two adhesives for his work—a temporary and a permanent one. There are so many brands of adhesives on the market from which to choose, probably no one outside the business is familiar with them all. However, a discussion of the five most-used types may help in making a selection.

Rubber Cement

The temporary adhesive the craftsman will need is rubber cement. It is used in any situation where pieces are to be held together during a particular operation, then separated. When the work has been done and the pieces separated, the cement left on the material is easily removed by rubbing the surfaces briskly with the fingers until no trace of it remains.

Although rubber cement is most often used for attaching patterns to wood, or for fastening two pieces of wood together during a sawing operation, it comes in handy in many other ways. If very small pieces are to be carved and sanded, as mentioned earlier, rubber cement can be used to fasten them to a larger piece of wood or heavy cardboard. They can then be worked on much more easily than if held with the fingers. Also, if such pieces are to be sprayed with material from an aerosol can, attaching them with rubber cement to a newspaper will prevent them from being blown away or turned over during the process.

Rubber cement dries quickly and for this reason also becomes overly thick after a period of time, especially if the container is only half full. A supply of benzol or rubber cement thinner should therefore be kept on hand. Trying to mix the thinner with the cement is difficult but unnecessary. If the thinner is poured on top of the cement and the container closed and left to stand overnight, the two will blend together automatically.

White Glue

White glue is sold under a variety of brand names, the best-known of which is Elmer's. White glue is probably the most popular all-purpose adhesive on the market. This water-soluble glue is easy to use, has strong holding qualities, dries rather quickly, and becomes transparent when dry. This transparency, however, does not make white glue invisible. As with all other adhesives, any excess left on the wood should be removed immediately.

One method of using white glue that will minimize the chances of a squeeze-out around the joint is to cover both glueing surfaces thinly with the adhesive and allow them to dry for a minute or so. A thin line of glue is then placed along the center of one of the surfaces and the two pieces clamped together. If one edge of a joint will not show in the finished piece (such as the inner edge between the side and top of a cabinet), the line of glue should be placed along that edge instead of in the center so that if squeeze-out does occur, it will be concealed inside the cabinet.

In most cases, white glue is sold in plastic containers with pointed tips which can be used to apply the adhesive directly to the work. The small 1 ¼-ounce container is the most convenient size to use for this purpose, but the large 16-ounce size is by far the most economical. To combine both assets, it is a good idea to buy one of each size, and to keep the small container filled from the larger one.

Epoxy

Epoxy is a permanent adhesive which, if used under the proper conditions, will bond porous surfaces together so tightly they can never again be separated. Most other adhesives form a bond through a process of drying. Epoxy does not dry; it sets as the result of a chemical action, and the lengths of the setting times are built into the adhesive during its manufacture. One can therefore select the epoxy whose setting time best suits his purposes.

An epoxy that sets in five minutes is ideal for the maker of miniature furniture. For one thing, it solves the problem of having to hold small pieces with the fingers until the adhesive has hardened. In its most practical form, epoxy is sold in two tubes from each of which an equal amount is mixed thoroughly prior to use. The setting time starts from the moment of mixing. If about two minutes are used for mixing and applying the adhesive, the pieces to be glued need to be held in position with the fingers for three more minutes only.

Epoxy can do certain jobs that no other adhesive can do as well. If two flat pieces are to be glued together, for example, and one of them is slightly warped, epoxy will hold it flat against the other permanently. The curve in a piece of wood is so persistent, it may return in time if other, less permanent, adhesives are used.

An exact setting time of five minutes for 5-minute epoxy can be counted on only when an equal amount from each tube is used. If a slight excess of hardener (in the black-capped tube) is used, the setting time will be shortened. It will be lengthened if more than half of the mixture is composed of material from the red-capped tube. These slight differences in setting times are not very important, however. If the craftsman makes an effort to squeeze equal amounts from each tube, he will not be very far off.

When the pieces for which epoxy has been mixed have been clamped together, it is sometimes a temptation to use the rest of the mixture for something else. Even though the adhesive may still be thin enough to spread, this is not a good idea. If the mixture has thickened noticeably, it will not penetrate the pores of the wood and the bond will not be satisfactory. It is therefore best to mix a fresh batch for each operation and to prepare only small amounts at a time.

A convenient method for mixing small batches of epoxy is to squeeze dabs of the material onto a nonporous surface, such as a disposable aluminum pan, and to mix them thoroughly with a toothpick. The same toothpick can then be used to apply the adhesive to the wood.

Since freshly mixed epoxy has very little body, squeeze-out beyond the joint can be a problem. Extra care should therefore be taken not to apply it close to the edges of the glueing surfaces, and the warning is repeated that all excess should be removed immediately. Epoxy hardens to a clear, glossy surface that no stain can penetrate.

Epoxy Ribbon

Epoxy ribbon (also sold as epoxy putty) comes in the form of a flat, claylike ribbon which is composed of two colors running side by side. To use it, a piece of the ribbon is cut off with scissors and the two colors kneaded together until thoroughly blended. The result is a solid adhesive which will become almost hard in about an hour, and will be thoroughly set the next day.

Because of its instant holding quality, epoxy putty can solve many problems for the craftsman. It will hold a fairly heavy chandelier to the ceiling immediately; small balls of it can be used to hold pictures to walls and hooks on moldings without danger of squeezeout. It does a good, if not perfect, job of holding metal pieces together, and in general is a clean, easy-to-use adhesive.

The epoxy ribbons with which the writer is familiar come in combinations of blue and yellow, or gray and tan. The former seems to have a stronger holding quality. In addition, the blue and yellow, when kneaded together, result in an attractive deep green which is useful for making plant leaves and stems.

The material can be painted after it has set, or paste colors (including metallic paste) can be worked into it before it is used. However, the latter method of coloring undoubtedly weakens the material's adhesive quality, and should therefore be used only when decorative pieces are being made.

Contact Cement

Contact cement is a sticky substance which is applied to both glueing surfaces and allowed to dry for a few minutes. The two wood pieces are then pressed together for an immediate, permanent bond. Since hand pressure is sufficient, no clamps need be used.

Contact cement works so quickly that once large pieces of wood (or other materials) have been pressed together, no adjustment of their positions can be made. On very small pieces, however, the bond is less powerful and the pieces can be repositioned as necessary.

For use with miniature furniture, the writer feels that either epoxy or white glue is preferable to contact cement. Contact cement is useful, however, for bonding metal to wood, which the other adhesives cannot do satisfactorily. Whenever possible, metal pieces should be attached to wood with small brads or screws. When they are not so attached, contact cement will make a good, if not perfect, bond.

Duco Cement

Because it has a great deal of body, Duco Cement is useful for attaching a small, nonporous piece, such as a glass bead or metal trim, to wood. The adhesive forms a bed around the piece being glued which other, thinner adhesives cannot do. This same quality of thickness makes Duco useful for glueing very tiny surfaces, such as ends of chair arms and stretchers to the backs and legs of chairs.

As a general-purpose adhesive, Duco does a satisfactory job; furniture put together by the writer, years ago, with Duco is still intact. However, since white glue makes a stronger, more permanent bond and is just as easy to use, it is recommended that Duco be used only for special purposes.

Acetone, which will mar plastic surfaces, is the solvent for Duco, so the adhesive should not be used on plastic materials.

8

Finishing Wood

Finishing the wood of miniature furniture gives all the pleasure and none of the tedium involved in finishing full-size pieces. Within limits, the craftsman may do as little or go as far as he pleases in using stains, fillers, varnishes, lacquers, waxes and oils.

The minimum requirements are a thorough sanding, a filler where needed, a stain and a top coat. The stain may be applied before or after the filler.

Sanding
Whether the furniture is assembled before or after finishing, all parts must be carefully sanded before anything else is done. A medium-fine grit paper should be used first, followed by one of a fine or very fine grit.

All edges and outer surfaces should be sanded until they feel very smooth to the fingers. Glueing edges should be straightened with a file. The point of a small piece of sandpaper, folded into a triangle, is useful for reaching indentations in carving. Turned pieces, such as spindles and balusters, can be wrapped in a roll of

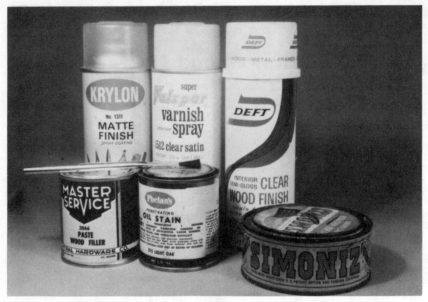

A variety of materials is available for finishing wood.

FINISHING WOOD

Mahogany is porous and needs filling.

sandpaper and smoothed by turning their ends with the fingers.

When sanding has been completed, a piece of tack cloth should be used to remove all dust particles from both the wood pieces and the surface of the worktable.

From this point on, there are no hard-and-fast rules for finishing the wood. A stain may be applied, followed by a filler, or the order of these two steps may be reversed. Whether to stain before or after filling is a minor debatable point as far as miniature furniture is concerned. On unbroken areas of full-sized furniture, changing the order of the two steps may somewhat alter the finished appearance, but makes no appreciable difference on small pieces. Since the most common practice is to use the filler first, this is the order in which they will be discussed here.

Thorough sanding is first step.

Filling

In general, hardwoods need to be filled, and softwoods do not. This does not always hold true, however. For example, the

All dust is removed with tack cloth.

most-used furniture hardwoods such as walnut, mahogany and oak, are open-pored and do need to be filled, but some other hardwoods, such as gum, hard maple, and birch, do not. Whether or not to use a filler should be determined by the appearance of the wood itself. If the pores can be seen or felt, they should be filled.

Although a variety of fillers is available, some in spray form and some combined with a top coat, nothing has yet replaced the standard paste wood filler for dependability. It is a putty-like material which is of about the consistency of thick cream after it has been thoroughly stirred in the can. If after a period of use it becomes too thick, it can be thinned with turpentine or benzine.

The color of the filler should match the color of the stain as closely as possible. Fillers of the standard wood colors can be purchased ready-mixed, and these may be blended together in any proportion to obtain other colors. Japan colors, available in paint stores, can also be used for coloring fillers.

Filler is applied against grain.

Filler wiped off against grain.

The filler should be applied with a fairly stiff brush and forced into the pores of the wood by brushing against the grain. It should be allowed to dry for eight or ten minutes until the surface shine has largely disappeared, then rubbed off, again against the grain, with a piece of rough cloth. Rubbing should be thorough so that the filler is left in the pores only; none should remain on the surface.

A second hard rubbing against the grain with a piece of soft cloth, such as cheesecloth, will leave the surface with a slight sheen and smooth to the touch. The filled pieces should then be set aside to dry overnight.

Staining

The craftsman has a selection of stain types from which to choose but, on small pieces, the subtle effects of using such materials as water stains and overglazes would largely be lost. Furthermore, since rings from wet glasses will not be left on the wood surfaces of miniature furniture, nor will scratches accumulate after years of use, materials to prevent these calamities need not be used. If the finished wood is smooth to the touch and has a nice color and luster, nothing more is necessary.

An ordinary penetrating oil stain is a good choice. It comes in a wide selection of colors; and it is easy to use since all it needs is a thorough mixing.

The stain should be applied with a brush, this time with the grain, and all surfaces, including backs, bottoms and the inside surfaces of doors and drawers should be covered. These more-or-less hidden areas need not be filled nor given a top coat, but their color should match the rest of the piece.

After the stain has dried for a few minutes, the excess is wiped off with a cloth, again with the grain. If the color is not as deep as desired, a second application may be made. After it has been stained, the wood should be very smooth and show the grain clearly. Hand-rubbing at this point will help to prepare the surface for the top coat, which should not be applied until after the stain has dried for the period recommended by the manufacturer.

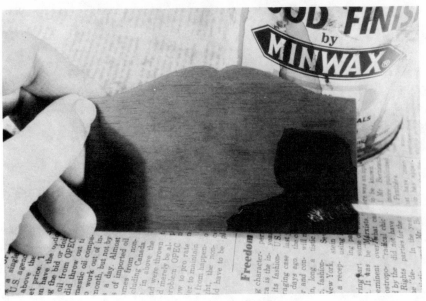

Stain is applied and wiped off with grain.

Top Coat

Depending upon the effect desired, the finishing coat may be lacquer, varnish, wax, oil, a combination of these, or one of the newer products such as a polyurethane finish. One modern product, Deft, is a combined top coat and sealer which, as a bonus, has enough body to fill small pores in the wood that the filler may have missed. It dries in a few minutes and, if not sprayed on too heavily, leaves an attractive, satin finish. Too heavy a coat, however, gives a shiny, enamel-like surface that deprives the wood of its character. A visit to any well-stocked paint store will acquaint the craftsman with what is available in both the standard and the newer finishes.

Because of the intricacies of miniature furniture, it is easier to cover hard-to-reach areas with a spray than with a brush, so when possible, choose material in spray form. This is especially true when working with lacquer; because of its fast-drying

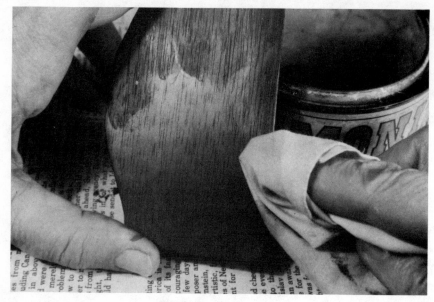

Finishing coat of wax.

quality, it is difficult to brush smoothly on any furniture, large or small.

Whether to give the miniature piece a top coat of varnish or a varnish-like material, or simply to finish with a coat of wax or oil, depends entirely on the craftsman's personal taste. In general, a simple oil finish looks well on most furniture of the seventeenth and eighteenth centuries, while pieces of later periods can be given a finish of a higher luster. No wood furniture should be given a high-gloss finish.

Although full-sized furniture is sometimes given multiple coats of varnish, one light coat is usually enough for small replicas. If more than one coat is applied, care should be taken that the material does not accumulate in areas where fine work, such as carving, has been done.

If desired, a top coat of varnish or similar material may be waxed as a final step. The craftsman would do well to experiment on wood scraps to learn just what material, or combination thereof, will give the wanted effect for any particular piece.

9

Assembling

If the same procedure used in furniture factories for assembling full-sized pieces could be used for miniature furniture, many of the craftsman's problems would vanish. Much of his enjoyment would also be gone, however, since putting together each new small piece is a puzzle to be solved and a challenge to be met. No two pieces of furniture present quite the same problems, and even the parts of two similar pieces, such as those of two chairs of different designs, might need to be assembled in an entirely different order.

The reader should keep in mind, then, that when a sequence of assembling parts is suggested in this chapter, it does not mean no other—and possibly better—ones exist. Any sequence that facilitates putting together a particular piece is the one to use.

Before the work of assembly begins, the craftsman should become familiar with some of the operations he may need to use as he goes along.

Dowels
Dowels are needed to strengthen joints when an adhesive alone cannot do the job. Such an occasion might arise when the glue-

ing surfaces are very small, or when a joint of extra strength is needed for a piece that will have no other support.

When used for this purpose, a dowel is a short stick of wood whose two ends are inserted into matching holes in the pieces to be joined. Although in carpentry a dowel should be perfectly round to fit the round hole, for miniature pieces it does not matter if it is somewhat flattened as long as it is thick enough for its two ends to need slight pressure when they are pushed into the holes. Any tiny spaces that might be left around the dowel will be filled with adhesive.

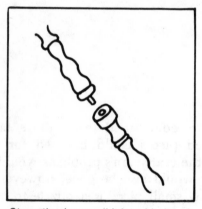

Strengthening small joint with dowel.

It is necessary that the two drilled holes be exactly opposite each other and, if two narrow posts are being joined, that they be in the exact centers of the ends. If one of them is even slightly off-center, the hole in the other piece must be drilled off-center to match it. Since this is extremely difficult to do, great care should be taken to measure accurately before drilling. The method for drilling holes is covered in chapter 6.

The dowel should be about ¼ inch long. It can be shaved from a larger piece of wood or cut from the end of a toothpick and sanded to uniform thickness. One end of the dowel is covered with adhesive and inserted into one of the holes. Adhesive is then applied to the other protruding end and to the glueing surface around it. The joint is completed by pressing the second furniture piece firmly into place. If the two surfaces do not quite meet, the dowel is too long and either its tip must be shortened, or its hole deepened a little.

Glueing Right-Angle Joints

When two flat pieces of wood are to be glued together at a right angle, a wood block, about 2 ½ x 2½ x 1 inch will prove to be an invaluable tool to the craftsman. One edge of the block is placed along the joint line, as illustrated, and the pieces pressed against the block's sides as the adhesive dries. This method will ensure an accurate right-angle joint.

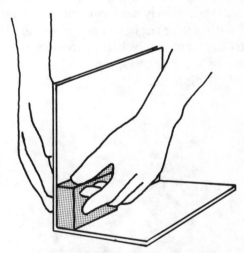

Using a wood block when glueing right-angle joints.

Flattening a Cut Surface

When a wood surface must be made perfectly flat and even, and it is too large to be straightened with a file, a piece of sandpaper should be laid on the worktable and the wood rubbed on it. Sanding the wood with paper held in the hand usually results in a slightly rounded surface which, while not always visible, may prevent a piece of furniture from standing straight.

Curving Wood

Within limits, small pieces of wood can be curved to fill special needs. The wood must be thin, cut so that its length runs with the grain, and its curve must be a gentle one. Because its grain runs in two directions, $\frac{1}{32}$- or $\frac{1}{16}$-inch plywood lends itself very well to curving. Flexible wood strips, available in shops that specialize in model train supplies, can also be easily curved. Any thin wood, however, can be slightly curved under the proper conditions.

The wood piece must first be soaked in warm water until it is thoroughly saturated. The time needed for this depends on the porosity of the wood, but any piece left in water overnight will be ready for shaping the next morning.

It is then curved, slowly and carefully, around a form and held in place with strong rubber bands or twine. The wood must be allowed to dry completely before the ties are removed. The form used may be a soda bottle, a jar, a can, or anything with a curve of the right diameter.

Rocking chair with shaped back.

A container with a tapering neck can be used for special curves. As shown in the illustration, the splat of the rocking chair is straight, but the side pieces of the back are curved in two directions; they curve forward so that their ends can stay fastened to the seat a little in front of the splat, and the whole back, excluding the splat, is rounded from side to side.

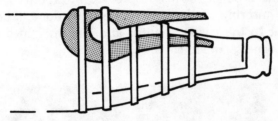

Back of rocking chair was shaped on soda bottle.

To make the back of the rocking chair, the neck end of a soda bottle turned out to be the perfect answer, since it allowed both curves to be made at the same time. The rubber bands which held the piece against the bottle were slipped under the splat so that its shape would not be changed.

When a special curve is needed that cannot be found on a ready-made container, a block of wood can be used. It is sawed in half along the line of the wanted curve and the wet wood is placed between the two halves. The halves of the block are then forced back together and tied firmly, as illustrated.

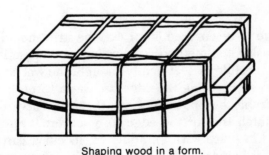

Shaping wood in a form.

Covering Edges

When an unattractive edge is exposed on a piece of miniature furniture, it should be concealed with a thin strip of wood. Because the three layers show at the edges, this is usually necessary only when plywood, more than $\frac{1}{16}$-inch thick, has been used.

Since the covering strips are very thin (about $\frac{1}{28}$ inch to $\frac{1}{32}$ inch) no mitering of the corners need be done. The strips are simply cut to the correct widths and lengths, glued into place, and the corners sanded smooth.

The 3/16-inch plywood edges of table's apron are concealed with a flexible wood strip.

If an edge to be covered is curved, the strip should be curved to match, using the method for curving wood described above. Where it is possible to tie it firmly enough, the wet covering strip may be shaped by using the edge itself as a form.

It is desirable but not necessary that the curve of the strip precisely match that of the edge to be covered. Since the strip will be held in place with an adhesive, its curve can be slightly altered as it is being glued. If the strip is thin and somewhat flexible, this presents no problem.

Shelves

Shelves are not at all difficult to make. The spaces for them are simply measured carefully and the shelves cut to size. Wood strips that are as narrow as possible and a little shorter than the depths of the shelves, are used as supports. Two supports for each shelf are glued opposite each other on the inner sides of the cabinet, with their back ends against the cabinet's back. For stability, the shelves should be glued not only to the supports, but to the sides and back of the cabinet as well.

Since there will be little strain on the glued joints, it is not necessary that the glueing be done on raw wood. It therefore simplifies the work if the shelves and cabinet are finished separately before the piece is assembled.

Pigeonholes

Any number of pigeonholes of any size can be made for a miniature desk by using a fairly simple method. The description of the operation is more complicated, actually, than the work itself. To make sure the principle is understood and measurements are correct, it may be helpful first to make a practice set of holes, following the accompanying illustrations and using heavy paper.

Pigeonholes are made of interlocking, slotted pieces similar to the dividers in some egg cartons and candy boxes. Although any desired number of holes and tiers can be made at one time, the principle will be explained on the basis of making eight holes in two tiers.

The length, depth, and height of the space which will contain the pigeonholes is measured first. Four pieces of wood are then cut: a horizontal shelf of the exact length and depth, and three vertical dividers of the correct height and depth.

Pencil lines are drawn on the shelf to divide it into eight equal spaces. The vertical pieces are similarly divided into four equal parts. It is important that the measurements be accurate.

The lines to be sawed into slots are then widened to equal the thickness of the wood being used. Care should be taken to widen them equally on each side of the drawn line, and they must stop exactly at the center line.

Making pigeonholes for desk.

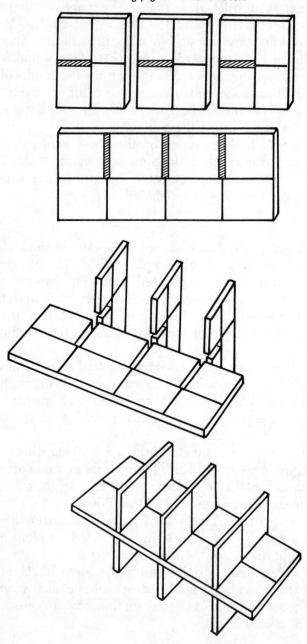

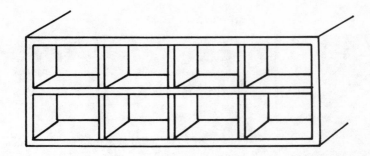

The slots are then cut with a saw and the pieces assembled as shown. The uncut cross lines on the horizontal piece are used as a guide for positioning the vertical dividers so that they are exactly parallel.

When the fit of the pieces has been tested, the pieces are disassembled, an adhesive is applied to the sawed edges, and they are glued together permanently. The pigeonholes can then be glued into the desk in one piece.

Shaped Edges

Unless the craftsman is making very early, or very modern, furniture, it would be almost impossible to complete more than two or three pieces without needing to shape an edge. If the edges are shaped on the model being used, eliminating this feature on the miniature copy would be a serious mistake. Shaped edges are one of the very important details that distinguish miniature replicas from toys.

Since a motor-driven shaper is not available for miniature work, some other way must be found to do the job. There are at least two methods which work very well.

The first and best method is shown in the illustrations. It will allow the craftsman to shape straight or curved edges in any manner he chooses. Two or three thin layers of wood are glued together to make the piece whose edges need to be shaped. Each layer should be of a slightly different size so that when the glueing is done, the edges will show the desired shaping. Depending on the edge wanted, the thickness of the layers may also be varied, as long as the total thickness is kept in scale.

SHAPING AN EDGE

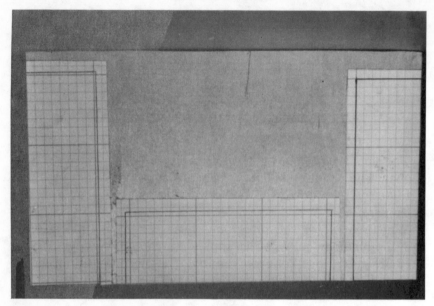

Patterns for three wood pieces of varying sizes.

Pieces are glued together.

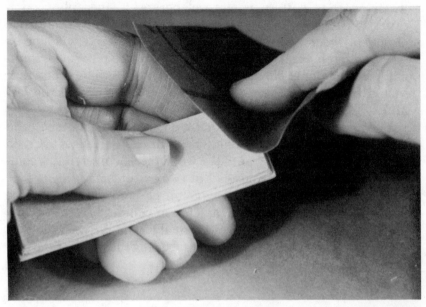

Thorough sanding of edges.

Top for table or chest, with shaped edges, ready for finishing.

Veneer may be used for the layers of straight-edged pieces, but when an edge pattern is more elaborate, $\frac{1}{32}$-inch plywood is easier to cut without danger of splitting. Since only a thin edge of the plywood will show, the color of its wood will not be distinguishable from the color of the rest of the piece after staining has been done. However, if the top layer is to be exposed, it should be made of the same wood used for the rest of the furniture.

The layers are fastened together with any strong adhesive and clamped tightly until the adhesive has dried. The edges are then sanded and rounded off until the wood piece looks as if it is composed of one solid layer instead of two or three.

The second method of shaping can be used only for a piece with straight edges such as a tabletop or cabinet base. A narrow file of any desired shape is used to make a lengthwise groove in the edge. This method was used for shaping the edges of the petticoat table shown here.

Top edges of petticoat table were shaped with file.

Beaded Edges

A beaded edge, where appropriate, adds a nice detail to furniture and takes very little time to make. The edge to be beaded is simply marked with pencil lines as illustrated. A line runs parallel to the edge of the wood to indicate the depth of the beading, and short, evenly spaced, perpendicular lines indicate the width of each bead.

BEADING AN EDGE

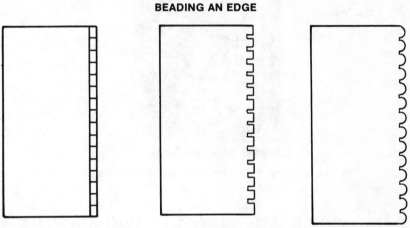

Equal spaces are marked on edge; saw cuts are made on drawn lines; file or sandpaper is used to round beads.

Cuts are then made between each bead by holding the wood piece exactly perpendicular to the saw's blade and by sawing to the marked depth. The beads are then rounded off with sandpaper or a thin file.

Assembling

Whether it be a chest, chair, or any other piece, a good rule to remember is that it is usually easier to assemble the more complicated parts first and to save the simple pieces for the last. When planning the work, however, the piece should be considered as a whole and certain preparations made before any glueing at all is done.

For example, if a dresser will need posts for supporting a mirror, it will be easy to drill holes for dowels on the top surface of

Beaded edge above doors of wardrobe adds nice detail.

the base after it has been assembled. On the other hand, after a delicate back has been attached to the seat of a chair, drilling holes for the legs, or for dowels to hold the legs, would be difficult. Necessary holes should therefore be drilled in both the bottom and top of the seat before assembly begins.

There are enough differences in the assembly of furniture of different styles to merit separate discussions of each.

Chairs

One very important feature of a chair, often ignored in dollhouse pieces, is the slant of the back. Except for those on chairs of a very early period, the great majority of chair backs are on a different axis from that of the back legs and slant slightly backwards. The difference between them is sometimes subtle, but a vertical or slanted back can determine whether a chair looks right or wrong, as shown in the illustration.

A chair back is attached either to the back edge of the seat or

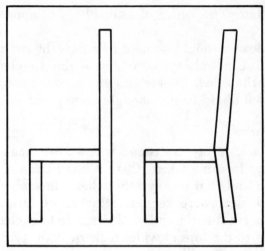

Nearly all chair backs should be given a slight backward slant.

to the back legs. Its glueing surface should be filed or sawed to the correct angle for the slant desired, and both an adhesive and dowels are used to hold it firmly in position.

In some chair styles the sides of the back are extensions of the back legs and are cut in one piece with them. In other styles the back legs may extend in a straight line a short distance above the seat. A shield-shaped back is then fastened at an angle between the extended legs. A study of pictures of chairs will show how various backs are styled and attached, and whichever one is selected for reproduction, all lines and angles should be copied exactly.

Since it is usually more delicate and complicated than the legs and stretchers, the top section of a chair should be assembled first. Holes for spindles—if needed—should be drilled in the seat and back frame and holes for dowels drilled in the frame where the arms will be attached. Where needed, holes are also drilled in the bottom of the seat for legs or for dowels, as mentioned above. The back is then assembled and attached to the seat.

The writer has found it convenient to add the legs next, and then the arm supports and arms. The stretchers between the legs are added last. This order of assembly is completely flexible, however.

Ideally, dowels should be used to attach the stretchers to the legs, but this is not always necessary. If the stretchers are cut a little longer than their final length and sanded to an exact, tight fit, they should hold firmly enough when glued into place.

Rocking Chairs

Sooner or later, every craftsman will want to make a rocking chair. Except for the rockers, there is no difference between its construction and that of any other chair. In such chairs of an early period, narrow rockers are attached by fitting them into deep notches cut into the ends of the legs. In later chairs, the legs are attached to the tops of wider rockers. Both styles are shown in the accompanying illustration.

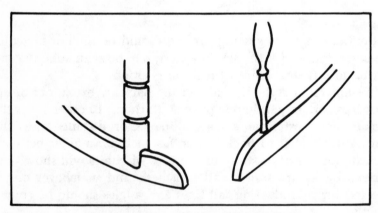

Attaching rockers of early and later periods.

Whether or not to use dowels when attaching rockers depends upon the sizes of the glueing surfaces. When the rocker is fastened in a notch in the leg, glueing is all that's needed. For legs fastened to the tops of rockers, dowels may be necessary, especially if the legs are quite thin.

For proper balance, ends of rockers always extend much farther beyond the back than the front legs. Correct positioning of the rockers can be copied from the model being used. It is enough to point out that balance is important, and that miniature rocking chairs should rock as evenly, if not as slowly, as do their larger counterparts.

Beds and Four-Legged Tables

The basic construction of a bed and four-legged table is much the same—vertical legs are attached to a horizontal platform. In both cases, the legs are usually thicker than are those of most chairs. While added strength can be given by drilling holes for the legs, or for dowels, this is not often necessary if epoxy is used on raw wood. If the headboard or footboard of a bed is in one piece with the legs, the work is made even easier. The end pieces are simply attached to the platform, and in this case, glueing surfaces are ample and no reinforcement is needed.

Since most styles of tables and beds are the easiest of all furniture pieces to make, they present no special problems, but do require attention to detail to make them attractive. In nearly every case, the edges of a table top should be shaped, and extra care should be given to finishing the top surface. The headboard and footboard of a bed are nearly always trimmed in some way, and every detail of the model should be included in the miniature copy.

The Victorian bed shown in the next chapter combines the use of cut-out, glued-on pieces, carving, curved wood, and knobs turned on a lathe. The headboard was made of two layers of wood, and the open, framed area was sawed from the top layer.

Pedestal Table

Because the legs must be inserted into notches in the pedestal, a pedestal table is a little more difficult to make than one with separate legs. If the pedestal is to hold three legs, notches for them must be cut by hand, using a sharp knife. When there are four legs, however, they oppose each other in pairs, and notches for each pair can therefore be cut on the jigsaw in one operation by using the following method.

Pencil lines are first drawn to divide the bottom of the pedestal

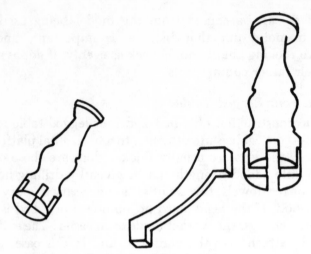

Sawing slots for pedestal legs.

into four equal sections as illustrated. Each line is then continued up the side of the pedestal to a distance equaling the length of the leg section that will fit into the pedestal. This line is next widened to the thickness of the wood used for the leg.

A space for two opposing legs can now be made by sawing a groove in the bottom of the pedestal as shown. The pedestal must be held very firmly against the saw's table, with one pencil line exactly on top and its opposite line directly beneath it. Accurate positioning of the pedestal in the saw is extremely important since the bottom line cannot be seen during the sawing. The two edges of the groove are then cut and the wood between the cuts cleaned out by moving the pedestal carefully from side to side and allowing the blade's teeth to file it away.

The work should be checked during the sawing to make sure the groove is in the exact center of the pedestal's base and that it is of the correct width for the legs. Pressure should be needed to insert the legs into the pedestal. If the groove is too narrow, it may be widened a little with a file, but if it is too wide, no amount of glueing can ever make the legs fit firmly.

Grooves for the legs of the world globe and piecrust table shown in the illustrations were cut into the pedestals by using the method described above.

Legs of world-globe and piecrust table were inserted into slots cut in pedestals.

Drawers

When the craftsman shows a piece of his miniature furniture, the one question he will hear over and over is, "Do the drawers pull out?" At times there is no real need for the drawers to pull out, but if they do not, he will have to face the discomfiture of having to say no. There is something shameful about a miniature drawer that does not work.

Making drawers and providing spaces for them is easy. The only real problem to be faced is that the cabinet or chest which will hold them must be left hollow. This makes the work a little more difficult. If none of the space inside the cabinet can be used, the only supports for the sides and back are the two back corners. If the wood used is thin enough to be in correct proportion to the scale, trying to glue unsupported corners solidly and at exact right angles can be difficult.

What is needed is an inside, perpendicular support at each back corner to which the sides and back can be glued. The sup-

ports should be at least $\frac{3}{16}$ inch thick and the same height as
that of the cabinet. If the cabinet were to have doors instead of
drawers, the space at the back taken up by the supports would
not be missed, but what can be done when both the supports and
the back ends of the drawers need to occupy the same space?

Following are three possible answers, and the craftsman may
think of others.

The first is that the drawers need not be quite as long as the
depth of the cabinet. This will leave room at the two back corners for the supporting posts shown in the first illustration.

**THREE WAYS TO SUPPORT
SIDES AND BACK OF CHEST WITH DRAWERS**

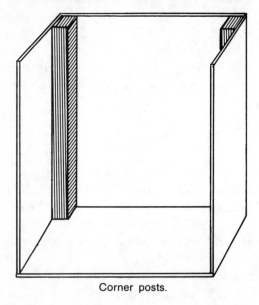

Corner posts.

Another solution is based on the fact that while the front corners of any heavy, stationary piece are always mitered, the
back corners are not. The back of such a piece is always sand-
wiched between the sides and, since it will not be seen, may be
of any thickness. If the back is made of $\frac{3}{16}$- or $\frac{1}{4}$-inch plywood,
its thick edges can then be used as a firm support for the sides as
shown in the second illustration. In this case, the drawers would

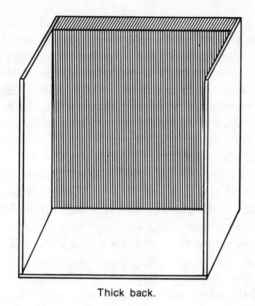

Thick back.

again have to be shortened to fit into the reduced space.

A third solution can be used only if the craftsman has an easy conscience. If there are to be many drawers, a few of them can be false, and the areas behind the drawer faces filled with solid blocks of wood to which the sides and back can be glued as shown in the last drawing. This is the easiest but least desirable method.

Wood blocks behind false drawers.

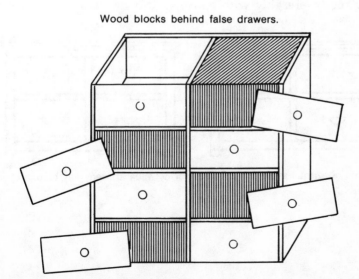

If supports are used, they are first glued to the back corners of the base. The posts must be placed far enough in from the edges to allow room for the sides and back which will be glued to their outside corners. In addition, although a base should be flush with the back of a cabinet, it is usually a little larger than the cabinet on the sides and front. This must also be taken into account when locating the supporting posts. When the posts are being glued into place, it is a good idea, if not necessary, to use dowels for reinforcement.

The back is then glued to the base and posts. The sides are added next and the top last. If a thick back is used instead of posts, the back is first fastened to the back edge of the base and the above order is used for assembling the rest of the piece.

The almost-hollow cabinet is now ready for shelves, dividers, and drawers. Although designs of cabinets and chests vary greatly, the shelves which support the drawers usually run the full width of the piece and the perpendicular dividers are placed between them. Occasionally it is the other way—the dividers are unbroken from top to bottom and the horizontal shelves are added in sections as shown. Either way, since supports would interfere with the drawers and therefore cannot be used, both shelves and dividers must be cut to fit the spaces so snugly they will stay in place even before an adhesive is applied. If supporting posts have been used at the back of the cabinet, thin strips of wood should be glued to the back edges of the shelves as stops for the drawers. The shelves and dividers are then glued into place, preferably with epoxy.

Either the horizontal shelf or vertical divider between drawers may be unbroken.

If measuring has been accurate, any slight difference in the sizes of the openings will not be seen. The drawer faces, however, must fit the openings exactly since a variation in the widths of the cracks around them will be very noticeable. Each opening should therefore be measured individually and a face cut to fit it.

Accuracy in the size of the drawers themselves is not as important as in the size of their faces. The drawers should be narrow enough to be able to slide in and out of the openings easily, but not so narrow that they can be moved from side to side.

Any wood, about $\frac{1}{16}$ inch thick, can be used for the drawers. The sides and back of a drawer should be glued to the outside edges of the bottom piece. The back corners need not be mitered; a thorough sanding to round them off is sufficient. The bottom should also be sanded smooth so the drawer will slide in and out easily. The front end is left open for the face.

The work of adding drawer pulls to the faces, or at least drilling holes for them, should be done before the faces are glued to the drawers. Since it is far more important that the faces line up with the lines of the cabinet, rather than with those of the drawers, the drawers are next placed in their openings, as illustrated. An adhesive is then applied to their front edges and

To ensure correct positioning, drawers are put into place before faces are glued on.

the faces positioned carefully and pressed against them. In this way, any flaw in positioning will be in the relationship between the drawers and the faces, where it will not show, and not between the faces and the cabinet.

10

Upholstering

Strictly speaking, upholstered furniture includes only pieces which, with the exception of legs and decorative touches, are entirely covered with upholstery material. Chairs and sofas with exposed wood frames are referred to as "partially upholstered." Although partial upholstering takes less time to do, furniture that is to be fully upholstered need not be constructed with the precision required for pieces with exposed wood, so there is not much difference between the work required for completing either an upholstered or a partially upholstered piece.

Whenever possible, sewing should be avoided for miniature work. This applies not only to upholstery material but to all other textiles as well. If the stitches were on the 1-inch scale, they would have to be so tiny as to be almost impossible to make. Moreover, even if they could be made by a particularly clever craftsman, 192 stitches to an inch (equal to 16, full-size), would make a stiff, unattractive seam or hem. It could be argued that no viewer is going to count miniature stitches so their exact number is unimportant. Although this is true, the eye very quickly picks up out-of-proportion details and the writer has not yet seen hand stitching on a miniature piece that looked just right. An adhesive, then (either white glue or Duco), should be used for upholstering miniature pieces.

Furniture to be Upholstered

When constructing a piece of furniture that is to be upholstered, only the lines and proportions need be considered. Since the material used will be entirely covered, it may be anything that can be easily cut and shaped. The writer would like to add, "with the exception of cardboard," but since this is largely personal prejudice, will refrain from doing so.

Because of the ease with which it can be worked, balsa wood is an ideal wood to use for such furniture. All the soft curves of a fully padded piece can be built right into the wood itself, and no extra padding need be used. In addition, if the craftsman wishes, a natural, inviting appearance can be given to a chair by sanding into the wood indentations in its back and seat. The chair will then look as if it has given years of comfort to its user.

Whatever the material used, the same attention should be given to line and shape that is paid to a piece to be only partially upholstered. The back should have a slight, backward slant and, unlike some all-wood chairs, its line should flow smoothly from the feet to the top, with no visible angle at the seat line.

Upholstery Material

As anyone who has been through the experience knows, selecting just the right material for upholstering full-sized furniture can be an ordeal. First in importance is usually the color; pattern is apt to be next; and weight and weave last.

When looking for material for miniature pieces, the order is much the reverse. The weight and weave are of first importance. The material should be thin enough so that turned hems will not be bulky, and the weave should be as fine as possible. The pattern may be anything as long as it is small enough, and if the shopper is lucky enough to find something that fills those first requirements, he will probably not hesitate to buy a length of fire-engine red instead of the blue he had hoped to find.

If a piece of material is too heavy and coarse, nothing at all can be done about it. It is possible, although difficult, to improve a too-large pattern with the use of textile paints. Changing the color of a small piece of material, however, can be done very easily.

Since the finished chair or sofa will not be exposed to sunlight, nor will its upholstery need to be cleaned every year or two, using fast textile dyes is not necessary. Almost any liquid that will give the approximate, desired color can be used. It may not always be possible to attain the exact shade wanted, but if a mixture of green ink and water will turn that bright red material into a soft brown, the craftsman can consider his dye job a success. Tea, coffee, water colors, vegetable juices, or inks can form the basis of a needed dye.

Dyes should be tested on scraps of material on a trial-and-error basis, and it should be remembered that colors will be lighter and much less bright when the material has dried.

To prevent the color from settling more heavily in one place than another, newly dyed material should be blotted between paper towels until partially dry. Although a nubby, unpressed look is sometimes attractive in upholstery, if it is not wanted, the wrong side of the material may be ironed while it is still slightly damp.

Some time ago the writer was fortunate enough to find an almost-perfect piece of material in a drapery shop. The tiny flowers and leaves were woven into it, the texture was right, but the color was pink. It was used as it was on the Victorian bed shown here, since the color was suitable for this piece of furniture.

For the sofa, also shown, a piece of the material was dipped into a cupful of liquid which combined green food color, India ink and water. By good fortune, the result was a soft, faded green with a muted pattern that bore no resemblance at all to the pattern on the bed cover. This material will be used again, in another color, when the need arises, and the writer's only regret is that only ⅛ yard of it was purchased at the time.

When searching for usable textiles, it is a good idea to look at the wrong side of the material as well as the right. The pattern on the wrong side is sometimes smaller and less sharply defined.

Bedspread material was dyed to make upholstery material for sofa.

This is especially true of polyester knits whose two sides are often completely different as the illustration shows.

The wrong sides of some materials can be used for upholstering.

Leather

Since methods for upholstering with leather are no different from those used for textiles, the requirements for the two materials are much the same. The leather should be supple and thin enough to be turned under without showing bulk, and there should be some stretch in it. Leather so thick it will not follow a curve or hollow is not suitable material for upholstering miniature pieces.

A thin kid glove makes excellent upholstery leather as does an artificial leather glove which is usually made of stretchable nylon or similar material. The latter is easier to handle than real leather, does not ravel, and looks genuine on miniature furniture.

Methods

In general, methods for upholstering or partially upholstering a piece are the same:

A paper pattern is cut.

A piece of backing material is cut a little smaller than the pattern.

Padding is glued to the backing piece.

Upholstery material is cut a little larger than the pattern and its edges are glued around the edges of the padded backing.

The padded, upholstered section is glued to the furniture.

Each of these steps is shown in the accompanying illustrations and will be discussed separately.

Cutting a Pattern

When upholstering is begun, the furniture parts have already been glued together as a rule and some areas to be covered (especially if their edges are curved) cannot be accurately measured. It may therefore be necessary to cut patterns for these parts on a trial-and-error basis. Using the original graph paper drawing of the furniture as a guide, the pattern is first cut a little larger than the area to be covered. It is then gradually reduced in size and shape by alternate trimming and testing until it fits the space perfectly.

A pattern should always be checked against the furniture itself, since even a simple, straight-sided section may not be exactly the same size in the finished, glued piece as it is in the drawing.

Backing

Using the pattern as a guide, a piece of backing material is next cut a little smaller all around than the pattern. The slightly smaller size of the backing will leave room for the upholstery material to be glued around the backing's edges without making the finished piece larger than the pattern.

Although backing upholstered sections is not absolutely necessary, it serves two useful purposes: the upholstery material can more neatly be turned and glued into a hem if it is fastened to a piece of backing rather than to itself, and if backing

PARTIALLY UPHOLSTERING A SETTEE

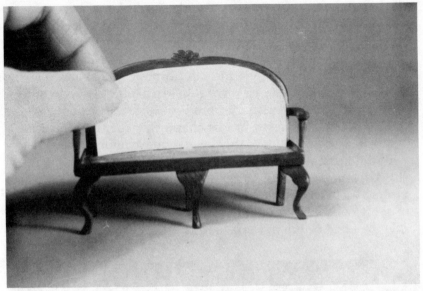

Paper pattern is cut a little larger than space.

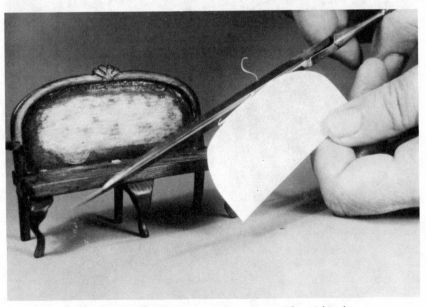

Pattern is shaped to fit by alternate measuring, trimming.

separates thin material from the turned-under hem, the ridge of the hemline will not show on the right side.

The backing may be of any thin material stiff enough to prevent the accidental turning under of its edge when the upholstery material is folded over it. A thin hair canvas (used for facing collars) is excellent for the purpose. Cardboard can be used or, if the upholstered piece needs to be flexible so that it can be shaped around a curve in the furniture (as was done at the foot of the couch shown in this chapter), paper may be used.

Since it is difficult to turn and glue comparatively heavy material around small curves of an unsubstantial backing a very stiff backing is needed for elaborately shaped sections. For such pieces, $\frac{1}{32}$-inch plywood is recommended. The pattern is glued to the wood, a sawing line is drawn a little less than $\frac{1}{16}$ inch inside the edge of the pattern, and the piece is sawed to shape.

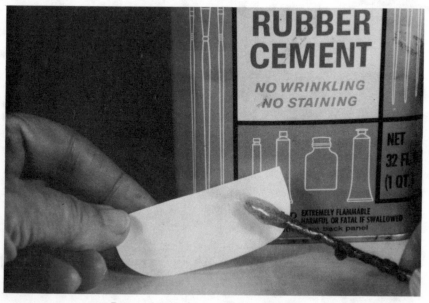

Pattern is glued to 1/32-inch plywood.

Padding

One very noticeable feature of many dollhouse chairs is that the padding is much too thick. When padding is called for on a

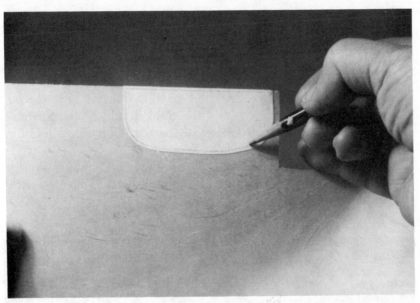

Line is drawn inside edge to allow for thickness of material.

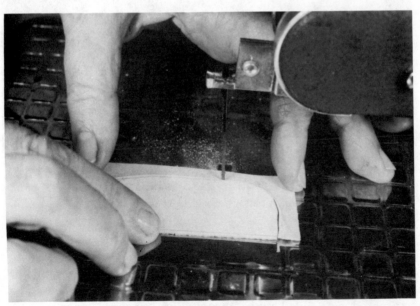

Wood backing is sawed to shape.

miniature replica, a sheet or two of thin cotton, a few layers of
facial tissue, or a single layer of cloth is usually sufficient. For
overstuffed pieces the padding should be a little thicker, but the
scale should always be kept in mind. It is better to err on the side
of too little padding than too much. When measuring the padding for thickness, the thickness of the upholstery material
itself should be considered, and the total should be proportion-
ately no more than the thickness of the seat or back of the full-
sized model.

A few dots of glue along the edges of the backing will hold the
padding in place, and the piece is then ready to be covered with
upholstery material.

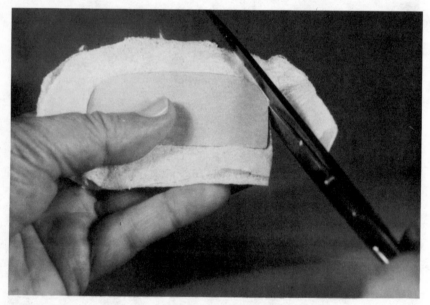

Cotton padding is cut to fit backing.

Adding Upholstery Material

A piece of upholstery material is next cut to the shape of the
backing and about ¼ inch larger all around. Since they can be
trimmed as needed when the glueing is being done, margins

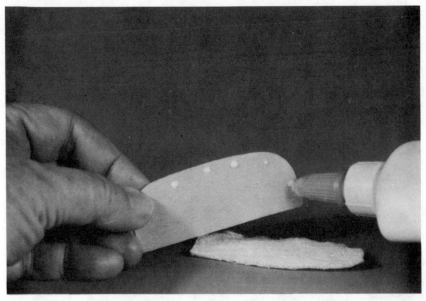

White glue tacks the padding to plywood backing.

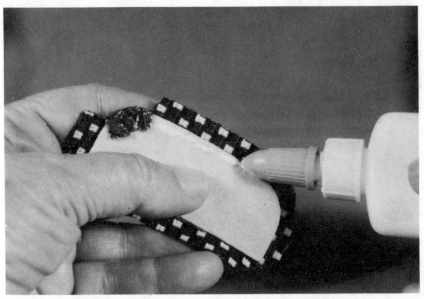

Upholstery material is glued to edges of backing.

With back finished, the same procedure will be followed for seat.

Partially upholstered settee, ready for guests.

should be ample so that there will still be enough left to work with on the opposite side if too much material is folded under one edge of the piece.

The edges of the upholstery material are then folded over the edges of the backing and glued into place, following the methods described in the next section.

Folding Corners and Curves

The simplest upholstered section is a square or rectangle that is glued to the back or seat of a chair. In most cases, the upholstered section is not quite as large as the furniture area it is meant to cover so that a margin of wood shows around its edges. However, if the upholstered section of a seat is the same size as the wood seat, the edges of the upholstered pieces are usually concealed by thin bands of wood. These bands, or aprons, cover the sides of the wood seat and extend a little above it to form a shallow "box" into which the upholstered seat is glued. The two chair seats shown in the illustration were handled in this way. In either case, the method for upholstering such a seat or back section is the same.

Shallow "boxes" hold seats for dining room chairs.

The way to fold the corner of a square or rectangular piece is shown in Figure 1. The corner is first cut off at an angle as shown in A. The cut should be about ⅛ inch from the corner of the backing. This ⅛-inch piece of material is then folded over the corner of the backing as shown in B and glued into place. In C and D the two sides of the upholstery material are folded over the backing and glued. The result is a mitered corner as illustrated.

FOLDING A CORNER

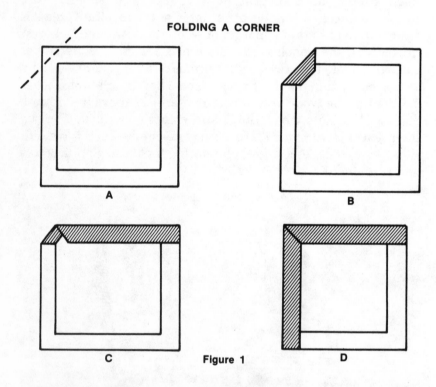

A

B

C   Figure 1   D

When a single piece of upholstery material covers not only the back or seat of a piece but the edges of the wood as well, the method for cutting and hemming the corners is shown in Figure 2. A slit is first cut in the corner, as in A. B shows a square cut out of the corner in order to narrow the edges that will be turned into a hem. The outer edges are next turned and glued as shown in C. The final step, D, is to hem the inside edges of the corner and to glue the upholstered piece onto the furniture.

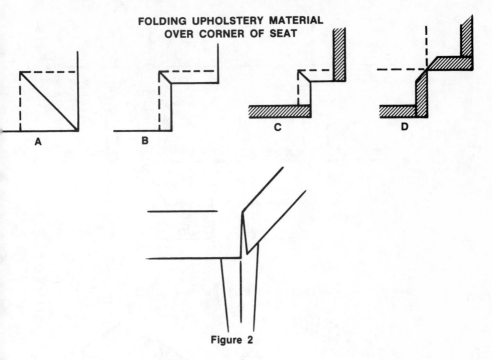

**FOLDING UPHOLSTERY MATERIAL
OVER CORNER OF SEAT**

Figure 2

When upholstery material is to be fitted around a leg or an arm support that is fastened to the straight side of a furniture section, the method is much the same, as shown in Figure 3. The material is first cut as in A. The edges to be hemmed are then narrowed by cutting out a section of the material as shown in B. The outer edges are next turned and glued, as in C, and D shows the final step of turning and glueing the inside edges.

For curved edges, the material should be snipped at intervals to the edges of the backing as shown in Figure 4. The distance between these cuts depends upon the sharpness of the curve; the sharper the curve, the closer together the cuts should be. These cuts will allow the material, when it is glued, to spread out and lie flat against the underside of the backing as illustrated.

Figure 3   FOLDING UPHOLSTERY MATERIAL
AROUND ARM SUPPORT WHERE IT JOINS SEAT

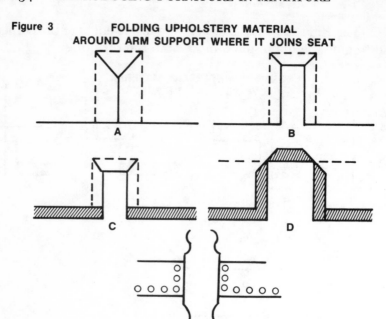

Figure 4   FOLDING UPHOLSTERY MATERIAL
AROUND A CHAIR BACK

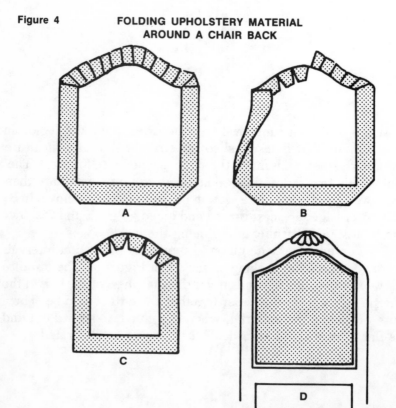

Seams

Although it is sometimes a temptation to upholster an area with one piece of material that is covered by two seamed pieces on the model, this should not be done. Every visible seam on the full-sized piece should be duplicated on the small copy by making as many separate sections as necessary. These sections are then glued to the furniture with their edges closely touching so that the lines between them appear to be seam lines.

The couch shown in the illustration was upholstered in this manner. Although it would have been easier to cut a single piece for the top surface and another for each side, the material was cut as shown so that all of the original seams would show.

Couch upholstered in artificial leather.

Edgings and Decorative Studs

Unless an upholstered section is set into an area with a raised rim around it, as described earlier, it is usually edged with narrow tape, cording, or a row of decorative studs. In addition, seam lines are often covered with cording.

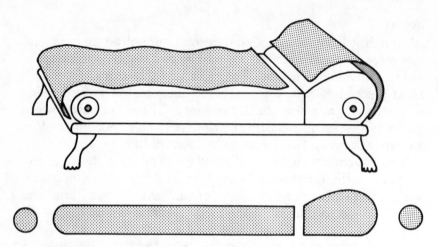

Upholstery pieces should be cut in sections to follow seam lines.

Since there is a fine groove between the sections into which the cording can be glued, covering miniature seam lines is a simple matter. Similarly, glueing a length of tape along the edges of an upholstered section is easy to do.

The only requirement for the tape or cording used is that it be in scale. An edging resembling tape can be made by lightly dabbing a few strands of embroidery thread with white glue, then pulling them through the fingers to distribute the glue, holding threads together to flatten them. If round cording is wanted, the glued threads can be rolled between the fingers. Other possibilities for tape or cording are the selvage of closely woven lace, heavy button thread, or string dyed to the desired color.

Studs, on full-sized furniture, help hold the upholstery in place. On miniature furniture, however, they are used solely for decoration and are added after the upholstering has been completed. Evenly spaced holes are drilled through the upholstery into the wood, and a short section of a pin or brad, including the head, is dipped into glue and pushed into each hole. Spacing the holes evenly is not difficult, but great care should be taken to make sure they are on a straight line. If even one stud is a slight fraction above the others, the eye will very quickly pick it out and the whole effect will be spoiled.

11

Accessories

There is nothing quite as enjoyable as furnishing a miniature room with accessories. One's imagination becomes more important than tools, and usable materials are everywhere. More often than not, the craftsman does not look for a piece of a certain shape to make a clock case, for example. The piece comes to him and demands to be made into a case which, up to then, he may not even have known he wanted. Accessories born of such happenstance very often turn out to be more original and attractive than those which have been planned.

It has been mentioned in an earlier chapter but is worth repeating here: any material at all can be used if its original purpose can be fully concealed. The last remark the craftsman should want to hear from a visitor is, "Oh, doesn't that earring make a cute wall lamp!" If he does hear it, the lamp should either be discarded or improved upon.

Since the imagination is unique and unpredictable, it would be impossible to cover fully in this chapter the subject of making everything out of anything. Only readily available materials and methods will be discussed for making the most generally used accessories. In addition, a few related but nonaccessory subjects have been included because it seemed the most logical place for them.

Marble

It would be ideal if real marble could be used for the tops of miniature tables, chests, and dressers. Correct proportions, however, must take precedence over everything else, and marble is too fragile to be cut properly thin.

A substitute that is almost impossible to distinguish from the real thing can be made of wood. Plywood of the proper thickness is excellent for this purpose, although any wood at all can be used. The steps described here for turning the wood into "marble" are shown in the accompanying illustrations.

The wood is first sawed to the shape and size wanted. Attention should be given to the details of whether the marble top on the model is a little larger or smaller than the wood top it is to cover (in some early furniture it is larger) and to whether or not its edges are shaped. If they are, the necessary pieces should be cut and glued together, following the method described in chapter 9.

The piece is then given a thorough sanding. Next, if the wood has an open grain, a neutral-colored, paste wood filler should be used and the surface lightly sanded again with a fine-grit paper. It is then wiped with tack cloth so that not a speck of dust remains.

The next step is to spray the top with several coats of a gloss or semigloss enamel paint, with time being allowed for thorough drying between each coat. If the background of the marble is to be a dark color, such as deep green, an enamel of that color should be used. A white or off-white enamel can be used for the background of marble of any lighter color.

When the last coat of paint has dried, the top should be as smooth as glass. If it is not, a very fine-grit sandpaper should be used and another coat of paint applied.

The piece is now ready to be marbled. A wood stain of any desired color such as brown, gray or green can be used alone or in combination. However, only the settled, oily pigment at the

MAKING "MARBLE"

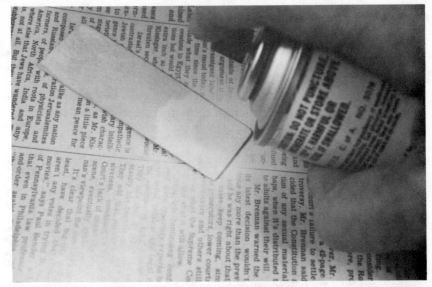

A coat of enamel paint is sprayed on.

Adding spots of oil wood-stain.

bottom of a can that has not been thoroughly mixed should be used. A little of the pigment is brought up on the end of a stick. A brush or the folded corner of a small piece of cloth is then used to dab the stain in scattered spots on the painted wood as shown in the illustration. With a clean piece of cloth the stain is then scattered irregularly, with quick, light dabs, over the top and edges of the wood as shown. With each dab, the marble grain becomes finer, so the craftsman may make areas of color as thin or as heavy as he wishes.

Dabbing stain with cloth.

Marbling a miniature top is something like doing a finger painting. The marble is finished when the craftsman likes what he sees. If, on the first try, this does not occur, the whole surface can be wiped clean of the stain with a piece of cloth and the work begun again. There is no reasonable limit to the number of times this can be done.

When the desired effect has been reached, the piece is left to dry overnight, although, since the stain cannot penetrate the enamel surface, it will not dry thoroughly. The advantages of

Marble grain becomes finer, lighter.

Coat of plastic-type spray protects pattern.

Marble ready to be glued onto furniture.

using an oil stain instead of paint are that it will not become tacky while being used, will not pile up to make an uneven surface, and will not dry too quickly.

The fact that it may never dry sufficiently to be safely rubbed with the fingers is a slight disadvantage that is easily overcome. A coat or two of any matte-finish, plastic-type spray will protect the pattern permanently.

Door Handles and Drawer Pulls

Although a limited variety of door handles and drawer pulls is available on the market, again the problem of proportion arises. If the 1-inch scale is being used, these pieces are useful for large doors and full-length drawers, but are out of proportion for smaller furniture parts. Since handles and pulls stand out conspicuously against dark wood, it is very important that they be in correct scale.

For a very small drawer or door, the simplest pull is the head of a brass pin or brad. A hole, a little smaller than the pin itself, is drilled in the wood, the pin is dipped in white glue and forced into it. The section of the pin inside the drawer can then be bent at a right angle with the fingers in order to give added resistance to future pulling. The bend should be made as close as possible to the wood. The last step is to clip the end short with wire cutters. If a brad is used, its end cannot be bent, but it can be made more secure by adding a small amount of epoxy to both the metal and the surrounding wood inside the drawer.

For larger handles or pulls, this basic pin-handle can be made more elaborate in a number of ways. For instance, a single link of a fine chain can be slipped between the pin's head and wood face. If the hole in the link is larger than the head, the link can be glued to the wood, around the head, with the use of Duco or contact cement.

A small bead, round or flattened, can be slipped onto the pin before it is inserted into the wood. A white bead is effective as a "porcelain" knob, while gold, silver, or clear glass beads make

MAKING DRAWER PULLS

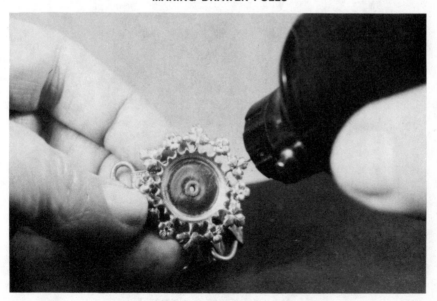

Holes for pins are drilled in flowers, leaves.

Pulls separated from jewelry piece with wire cutters.

Leaf pulls fastened to dresser.

pulls and handles that are remarkably similar to round knobs on full-sized pieces.

For more elaborate pulls, the craftsman's collection of old jewelry will prove to be invaluable. The accompanying illustrations show how a piece of jewelry, originally saved for a possible picture frame, furnished eight pulls. Alternate leaves and flowers made up the design of the circle's edge. In order to simplify the work, holes for pins were drilled in the flowers and leaves before they were separated from the center piece with wire cutters. The leaves were then fastened with pins to the drawers as shown and the flower pulls saved for some future piece.

Although the remaining center disc no longer suggests a picture frame, with the filing of its edges a small gold plate for candy may have been created.

Rugs

Miniature rugs, like all miniature furniture and accessories, must be in correct proportion to the scale. In many of the best dollhouses one sees hand-hooked, braided, and needlepoint rugs that are truly works of art. Some of them must have taken long weeks and months to complete and are a much-admired attraction in dollhouses. The fact that most of them would be several inches thick when transposed into full-sized measurements, detracts nothing from their charm.

The reader of this book, however, is to be allowed no such happy privilege. Even if his rugs must be made of newspaper, they should be of the correct thickness. If he would like to play a little game, let him first guess the thickness of a few of the rugs in his own home, then measure them. The imported wool broadloom that must be at least 1 ½ inches thick, measures less than ½ inch, and the pad ¼ inch. The shag rug in the hall with the very long strands is surely 2 inches thick, but proves not to be. Its flattened strands may feel thick to the feet, but stand not much higher than do the erect threads of the broadloom.

A full-size rug an inch thick is therefore uncommon and, transposed on the 1-inch scale, even such a rug would be only $\frac{1}{12}$ inch thick. The average rug would be half that.

The writer realizes that the idea of making a beautiful needle point rug will die hard with many lovers of fine miniatures and does not wish to discourage them. It may be possible to make one of the correct thickness with fine embroidery thread, a very thin backing and extraordinarily good eyes. However, there are any number of other possibilities, some of which will be discussed here.

Rag Rugs

Two simulated rag rugs, $\frac{1}{32}$ inch thick, are shown in the illustration. They are made of embroidery thread of assorted colors, whipped together on the back with needle and thread. Such a rug is started at the center in either a round or oval shape, and the thread sewn in a spiral until the desired size has been reached. The colors of the bands, which should vary in widths, are changed by cutting the thread of one color, folding its end to the back, and whipping in the start of the next one. When the rug is large enough, the last thread is cut, folded to the back and whipped into place. Using a steam iron, the rug should then be pressed flat on the underside.

It may come as a surprise to learn that starting with an oval center and adding thread evenly around the edges will still result in a round rug. To maintain the oval shape, a short length of thread must be added at each end on every round.

"Rag" or "braided" rugs made of embroidery thread.

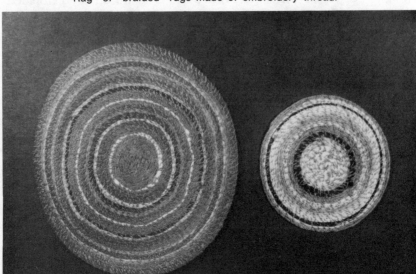

Oriental Rugs

An "oriental" rug which contains every fine detail of the original can be made from a picture cut from a book. When placed in a miniature furnished room, it looks entirely authentic and invariably draws questions as to its source.

MAKING AN "ORIENTAL" RUG

Picture cut from book is given heavy varnish coat.

There are several books in print, costing less than five dollars each, which contain many fine reproductions in full color of oriental rugs. Any chosen rug is cut from such a book along with a narrow margin around its edges. It is then "texturized" to minimize the printed look and dull its glossy colors.

Since it will be necessary to work quickly, the materials to be used must be assembled in advance. A single layer of white facial tissue (Kleenex seems to work best) is ironed to remove any small creases and as much as possible of the crease made by the fold. A spray can of varnish will also be needed. If varnish with a matte finish cannot be found, a semigloss or satin varnish can be used.

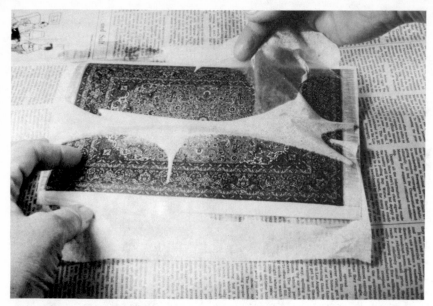

Facial tissue is quickly smoothed on.

Second, lighter varnish coat brings out colors.

The rug picture is placed face up on a newspaper, with the tissue within easy reach. It is then given a very heavy coat of varnish and the tissue immediately laid carefully on its surface. By pulling gently on the edges, as shown in the illustration, the tissue is smoothed until it is completely flat against the picture. If any bubbles have been trapped and cannot be released through the edges, they should be pricked with a needle and the area flattened with fingers. The tissue will absorb the varnish in a very short time, so the smoothing must be done as quickly as possible.

When the tissue-covered picture has dried, the colors, which were very bright while the varnish was wet, will have faded considerably, and the surface will have a dull, cottony look. However, another coat of varnish will bring the colors back. This second coat should be just heavy enough to wet the tissue thoroughly, but not so heavy that the tissue cannot absorb it all. For this coat, it is better to spray too lightly rather than too heavily. If excess varnish remains on the surface, the rug will have a shine and will have to be discarded. If too little varnish

Edges are trimmed.

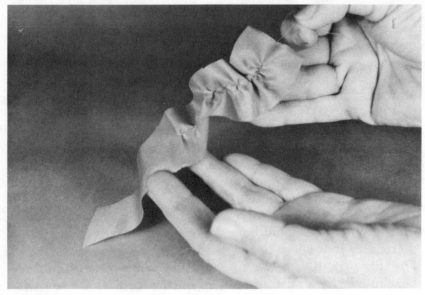

Making fringes—thread is pulled.

has been given, however, the rug will show light areas on drying, and these can be lightly spot-sprayed until they disappear.

When the rug has dried completely, the margins and printed fringes, if any, are trimmed away as illustrated. The cutting should follow the curved lines along the edges, since the slight irregularity will add to the rug's natural appearance.

Following the method described next, fringes are added to the ends and, as a final step, the rug is backed with any cloth of in-scale thickness. The backing should be cut about $\frac{3}{32}$ inch smaller all around than the rug and fastened to the underside of the rug with white glue. The narrow, unbacked edges of the rug are then curved slightly over the edges of the backing as shown.

Fringes. To make fringes, narrow strips of cloth are glued to the rug's edges, then raveled. The texture of the cloth used should be in keeping with the kind of rug for which the fringe is intended. A wool or cotton rug would have a somewhat coarser fringe than would an oriental or velvet rug. For the former, a fine cotton or

Cloth strips are glued to rug ends and trimmed.

Cross threads are pulled to make fringe.

Cloth backing adds body.

Completed, "texturized," Oriental rug.

wool material may be used; for the latter, a thin silk or polyester lining material works out very well. Whatever the material, it should be of a weave that ravels easily.

As a rule, fringes should be of such neutral colors as gray or beige and should not, in any case, be bright enough to draw attention from the rug itself.

To make two end-fringes, a strip of the selected material is cut a little longer than the width of the rug and about 1 ½ inches to 2 inches deep. The cross threads of the material should run with the width of the rug. A thread is then pulled in the approximate lengthwise center of the strip, as illustrated, and the material cut along the pulled line.

A thin layer of white glue is next spread along the ends of the rug, on the underside, and the cut edges of the material (the edges straightened by the pulled thread) are glued to them. In order to make the fringe threads lie perfectly straight, the material must be glued in a line exactly parallel to the end line of the rug. Care should be taken not to allow any of the glue to spread onto the material which extends beyond the end of the rug, since this would prevent the fringe from raveling properly.

The material is next trimmed short, to the desired length of the fringes, as shown in the illustration, and the ends cut flush with the side edges of the rug. The final step is to pull the cross threads out, as shown, leaving the completed fringes.

If a thicker fringe is wanted, two layers of cloth strips can be glued to each rug edge instead of one.

Wool Rugs

A piece of thin wool cloth of a dark color and fine weave can be made into a rug which makes an effective, muted background for miniature furniture. If the material is very soft, it should be backed with a thin material to give it body. A nylon mesh, or even a thin sheet of paper, can be used. The edges of the rug are folded over the backing, fastened with white glue, and pressed flat on the underside with a steam iron. Fringes may be added to the ends and, where appropriate, along the sides.

Dollhouse Rugs

Some manufactured dollhouse rugs are thin enough to be in keeping with the 1-inch or ¾-inch scale. More attention is being given now to detailed patterns in such rugs, and some of them can be used just as they are. Others may need to have their too-coarse fringes replaced with finer ones, and possibly more details added to their designs. This can be done with the use of textile paints and a fine brush. Unless the craftsman is experienced in the use of such paints, adding straight lines or symmetrical patterns should be avoided, but painting tiny flowers, leaves, or dots of color in open spaces is not at all difficult to do.

Hinges

Miniature hinges, to be in correct scale, can present a problem to which there is no easy solution. If the 1-inch scale is being used, manufactured hinges are sometimes available in shops that specialize in miniature accessories. If ready-made hinges cannot be found, or if any other scale is being used, they must be made by hand, or substitutes found for them.

For any single piece of miniature furniture, probably only one of three types of hinges will be needed, all of which are shown in the illustrations. The first is the decorative "leaf" or "strap" hinge which is fastened flat to both the door and frame so that the whole hinge is exposed. Because all the work of fastening is done on the face of furniture, the leaf hinge is the easiest to attach.

The second is the more commonly used "butt" hinge, of which only the joint is exposed. The plates which are fastened to the wood are concealed between the edge of the door and the door jamb. To install such a hinge, a small section of wood must be removed from both the door edge and jamb so that the plates will lie flush with the wood. An examination of any room or closet door will show how such hinges are attached.

The third type is the "offset" hinge designed for a lipped door (one whose edges slightly overlap the opening). Doors of wood cabinets in kitchens are typically supported by offset hinges.

To make any of the three hinges, a double-headed pin is needed, as shown in the illustration. Since the craftsman is not

THREE POPULAR STYLES OF HINGES

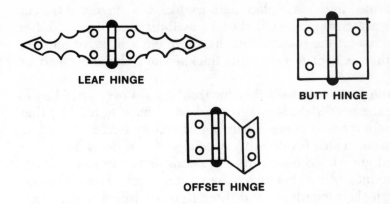

LEAF HINGE

BUTT HINGE

OFFSET HINGE

likely to find such a pin of the correct thickness and length, he can use an ordinary silver- or gold-colored pin, cut it short, and add a drip of solder to the cut end to make the second head. The solder drop can then be painted to match the pin.

MAKING A HINGE

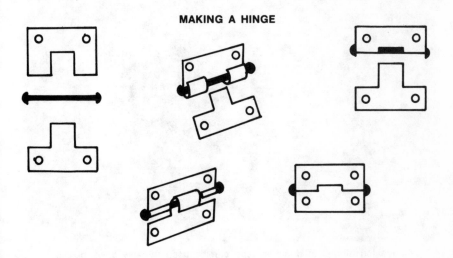

The shape shown in the illustration for the type of hinge needed is next cut from a thin sheet of brass, copper, tin, or aluminum. The metal should be thin enough to be cut with scissors, but thick enough to hold its shape when bent. Holes are next drilled in the face plates, after which the tongues of the cut pieces are curved around the pin as illustrated. For an offset hinge, one of the plates which has been cut a little longer than the other, is bent to match the thickness and shape of the door edge.

If the craftsman feels that his troubles are over after he has made the needed hinges, it is too bad to have to tell him that there are more to come. Fastening miniature hinges securely to thin wood can be difficult, especially if the doors are to be opened and closed constantly. The ends of pins or small brads, dipped into white glue, epoxy, or contact cement, and inserted through the hinge holes and through holes drilled in the wood will hold the doors on their hinges if they are opened only occasionally and with care.

Concealed hinges of gummed tape can be used for very small pieces.

Small pieces of gummed cloth or metal tape, fastened to the inside of the door and frame where they will not be seen, will give added strength to doors hung with hinges. This tape will prevent the doors from being swung wide open (which should not be done in any case since it puts an unnecessary strain on the hinges). If the doors are so small that metal hinges cannot possibly be used, the tape can be used alone.

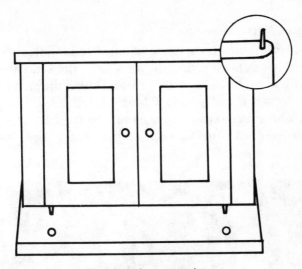

Hanging doors on pins.

There are two alternatives to using conventional hinges. A door may be hung so that it will pivot on short sections of pins inserted in the top and bottom edges as illustrated. Matching holes, into which the pins will fit, are drilled into the top and base of the cabinet. If this method is used, the edge of the door must be rounded off with sandpaper so that it can swing freely without being stopped by the frame. Also, since the pins would prevent it from being put into place later, the door must be added when the furniture piece is assembled and glued.

The second alternative to hinges (one which the craftsman would have thought of sooner or later himself) is to fasten the door in place temporarily with rubber cement, with the intention of removing it and adding hinges at a later date. It is a stopgap method, and of course the door cannot be opened; but it will soothe the craftsman's guilt feelings to know he can fix it later. In addition, visitors who ask if the door really opens will be satisfied to hear, "Well, not yet, but it will as soon as I can find the right hinges." Since adding tiny, workable hinges can present such a problem, this solution is not offered as facetiously as it may sound.

Picture and Mirror Frames

Sources of miniature frames are so numerous that, short of furnishing an art gallery (which is an idea!), the craftsman is apt to end with more than he can ever use. One of the richest sources is his collection of old jewelry. Many small buckles, brooches, earrings, and miscellaneous pieces can be used for frames after extraneous pieces of metal, such as pins and clasps, have been removed.

Any collection of old jewelry is a rich source for picture frames.

In addition, any shop which sells dollhouse accessories is usually well stocked with frames of wood, metal, plastic, or a composition material. Those of wood which the writer has seen lacked detail and were too thick to be correct for any scale; they could be better made by the craftsman at home. Some of the metal and composition frames, however, are well "carved" (by a molding process) and much can be done with them.

If the purchased frame is of pot metal or lead, there are usually unwanted ridges of the metal left along the edges by the casting. These should be filed or sanded off. The frame can then be painted and used as is, or embellished as desired. Tiny vines and leaves made of Polyform can be added and the whole baked in a slow oven. It can then be gilded, or painted black or brown, and the high spots burnished with a gold paste.

A small frame can be nested inside a larger one to give a rich effect. The illustration shows such a combination. The manufactured, rectangular frame is of a composition material and the

Small frame nested inside larger one gives rich effect.

small oval frame is a piece of jewelry whose original purpose has long since been forgotten. For the backing, a fine-grain pebbled leather is used as shown. The shine of the metal oval has been toned down by a coat of the same gold paint that was used on the frame and backing.

Wood Frames

A flat, wood frame of the type used for a watercolor or etching can very easily be made by first making an inside cut (described in chapter 5) to shape the interior of the frame. The outer edges of the frame are then sawed to shape.

If a thicker frame is wanted, however, its edges should be shaped. To do this, the same method is followed that is explained in chapter 9 for shaping the edges of a tabletop—two or three pieces of thin wood, of slightly different sizes, are sawed and glued together. The glueing must be done carefully so that the margins between the pieces are of the same width all around.

The illustrations show a method for making a frame with shaped edges and, if desired, for mitering the corners. Three pieces of wood of different sizes are cut as shown in Figure 1. In Figure 2, they have been glued together and a hole drilled at Point A through which the saw blade will be inserted in preparation for making an inside cut. At this point, if mitered corners are not wanted, the wood inside the frame is removed with an inside cut and the frame is ready for finishing and backing. To miter the corners, the cuts are made from Point A to each corner as shown. These cuts must be made outward, since it would be very difficult to start exactly at the outside corners and saw inward. The inside edges of the four sections (A, B, C, and D) are then cut as shown in Figure 3. Finally, the pieces are glued together at the corners and to a piece of backing material at the same time. The completed frame is shown in Figure 4.

Backing a Frame

If the picture to be framed is fairly stiff, its edges may be glued directly to the back of the frame. If it is of thin paper, a paper of light cardboard backing, cut a little larger than the opening in the frame, may be used; the picture is glued to the backing and the backing to the back of the frame.

However, for a heavy picture or mirror which is to fit inside

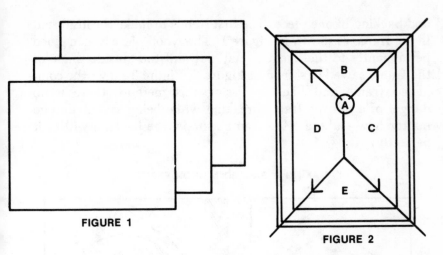

FIGURE 1

FIGURE 2

FRAME WITH SHAPED EDGES AND MITERED CORNERS

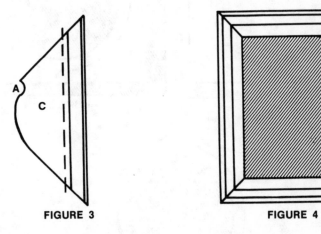

FIGURE 3

FIGURE 4

the frame, the backing should be very sturdy and is best made of thin wood. Since such a backing will be thicker than one made of paper or cardboard, its edges will show if they are not concealed in some way. The best method for concealing them is to cut the backing to match the exact size of the frame so that its edges become a part of the frame itself.

The illustrations show a simple method of cutting the frame

and backing in one piece. The first step is to make the inside cut in the frame as shown in Figure 1. The wood piece is then glued permanently to the backing material and the outside shape of the frame sawed as shown in Figure 2. Figure 3 shows the completed frame and backing. Using this method, there is no danger of a narrow frame breaking while being sawed, and no matter how elaborate the frame's shape, the backing will fit it perfectly.

MAKING A BACKED MIRROR FRAME

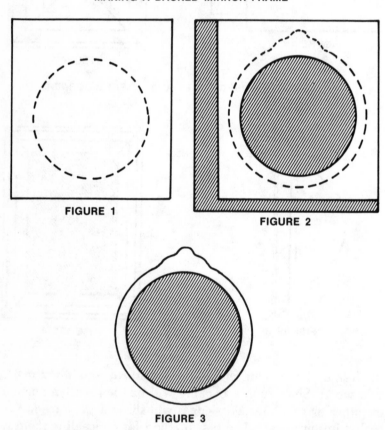

FIGURE 1

FIGURE 2

FIGURE 3

Figures 1–3: Inside cut is made; wood piece is glued to backing material; outside shape is sawed.

All frames, unless they are glued to backing material, should be supported by a piece of wood while being sawed, as described in the section on sawing thin wood in chapter 5.

Pictures

Even more plentiful than materials that suggest frames are those that suggest pictures to be framed. Many gift catalogs advertise paintings, etchings; and prints which are, for ordering purposes, reproduced in miniature, in the catalog. Home decorating and art magazines often show framed pictures that are small enough to be in the right scale for miniature rooms. The only requirement of any printed picture is that its colors be clear and true.

Small pictures, for framing, are plentiful in magazines and catalogs.

Reproductions of watercolor paintings, prints, and etchings may be left as they are and framed behind a sheet of thin, stiff plastic to represent glass. The surfaces of printed oil paintings should be thickened and roughened by applying a coat of clear nail polish, varnish, or plastic-type coating, and by dabbing the material with the fingers as it dries. For family photographs, faces of the correct sizes may be cut from group pictures and put in small oval or rectangular frames. Cardboard or wood supports are then glued to the backs.

Original oil and watercolors may be painted by the craftsman if he is thus talented. Fine handkerchief linen, coated with sizing to give it body, makes an excellent "canvas" for oils, and a very fine-grain paper will be suitable for watercolors. Such hand painting, however, should be expertly done. It is far better to use a printed picture than to hang one that lacks detail and the professional touch.

Clocks

Methods for constructing wood clock cases are no different from those used for making any other container or cabinet. Ceramic or porcelain cases can be molded of Polyform or clay, painted, and given a finishing coat of varnish or nail polish. Unless the craftsman has special equipment for working with metals, metal clocks can be made from odd pieces of jewelry or other shaped metal pieces, modified to suit a needed design.

The only clock parts which have not yet been discussed are the dials, the hands, and in the case of a grandfather clock, the weights, chimes, and pendulum.

Wristwatch dial is ideal for mantel clock.

For a dial, the best source by far is the dial of a very small wristwatch. A larger watch dial is apt to be unsuitable for either a ¾- or 1-inch scale. If the craftsman will pass the word around that he would like to have any old wristwatches which are beyond repair, he may be surprised at the number that will be brought from catch-all drawers where they were dropped years ago. No matter how hopeless its condition, there is something about an old watch that encourages hoarding and, unless it is solid gold, its owner is usually relieved to see it put to good use.

To remove the dial from such a watch, the hands must first be pried off. Since they are very thin and easily bent, great care must be taken in doing this. Pressure should be applied only at the center, next to the spindle, and never along the lengths of the hands. Caution should be used since watch hands are fastened on very securely and are apt to fly into the air as they are released. Although they stand out clearly against the light dial, they are so tiny as to be almost invisible against a dark ground. They should therefore be pried off in a box or similar enclosed space to keep them from disappearing forever.

Once the hands have been removed, the dial comes off rather easily. It can then be glued into place on the clock, and the hands glued onto it. The hole in the center of the dial (where the spindle had been) is so tiny it will not be seen after the hands have been replaced.

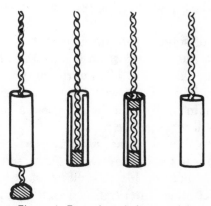

Figure 1. Fastening chain to weight.

The chimes and weights for a grandfather clock can be sawed in wanted lengths from hollow brass tubes of varying diameters (again, found in hobby shops) and their ends filed smooth. The chimes can be glued to the back of the case, but the weights should be suspended by thin chains. One method of fastening the chains to the weights is illustrated in Figure 1. The chain end is dropped through the weight and a small ball of some pliable material which will later harden is fastened to it. Epoxy can be bought in both paste and clay form, and either of these is excellent for the purpose, although, again, Polyform can be used. The clay ball, holding the chain end, is then pushed into the lower end of the tube, as shown, and packed tightly. A similar ball is packed in the upper end of the tube to hold the chain in the center of the opening. The weight is then laid aside to set or dry (or bake) for the period recommended by the manufacturer of the material used.

The next step is to fasten the other end of the chain to the ceiling of the cabinet, and this can present a problem. A grandfather clock is made in three sections—the base, the center case, and the top section which holds the dial and works. The top surfaces of the base and middle section must be perfectly flat so that the next section above will be level when glued to it. Since a weight is comparatively heavy, just glueing its chain to the ceiling of the cabinet is not sufficient, and the chain end cannot be fed through a drilled hole to the above surface as this would prevent the top section from remaining parallel to the rest of the case.

One method of solving the problem is shown in Figure 2. A hole is drilled in the ceiling just large enough to hold the folded end of the chain, the hole is filled with epoxy and the chain inserted so that its fold is flush with the top surface. This method will hold the chain securely, although the craftsman may think of others that will work as well.

The pendulum should be hung so that it will swing freely. In the clock shown, the pendulum was made by soldering the head of a brass thumbtack to a long needle. A short length of button thread was fed through the needle's eye, its ends separated and held to the ceiling with small patches of glued cloth as shown in

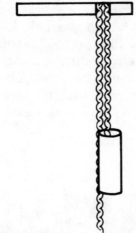

Figure 2. Attaching chain to top of clock case.

Figure 3. Since the needle's eye faces the sides of the case and is partially concealed by the door frame, it does not show.

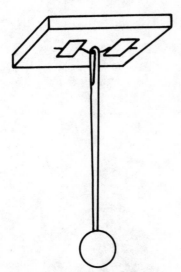

Figure 3. Attaching pendulum.

The dials on most grandfather clocks are backed by a square brass piece of the same size as the dial so that only its corners show. To make such a backing, a square is cut with scissors from a thin sheet of brass. It is then glued to a thin wood backing and its corners etched with a fine, pointed instrument such as a safety pin. The design of the miniature etching is so small as to be unimportant. It is enough that the surface of the brass be scratched in thin, curly lines, that the sides and bottom edges of each design be straight, and that equal margins be left all around.

Weights and chimes for grandfather clock were cut from hollow brass tubes. Thumbtack head, soldered to needle, makes pendulum.

The half-circles above the dials in some clocks can also be cut from a brass sheet. Some such areas show painted pictures and others indicate the phases of the moon. Either of these can be painted on with a fine brush and oil or opaque watercolors, followed by a thin coat of varnish.

For a dial so small that one from a wristwatch cannot be used, the worn-out battery from a hearing aid makes an excellent substitute. A paper circle is cut to fit inside the raised border and

Hearing-aid battery furnishes base of tiny "porcelain" clock.

the numerals and hands are drawn on it with black ink. The battery can then be put into a case of any wanted style or, by adding a bell and feet, it becomes a very convincing alarm clock just as it is.

Miniature Toys

There is no real reason for discussing miniature toys separately except that the temptation to do so is irresistible. Since it is not necessary to pay attention to such refinements as shaped edges, turned spindles and beautifully finished woods, making an occasional toy for a miniature playroom or nursery will serve as a vacation from the exacting work of making larger, more detailed pieces.

Christmas gift catalogs and reprints of old Sears, Roebuck catalogs are two excellent sources for finding toys to reproduce in

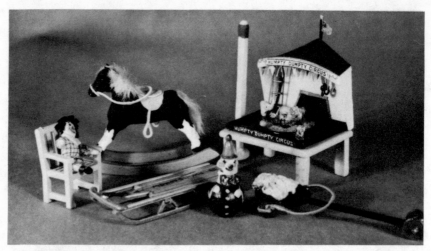

Making miniature toys furnishes a vacation from more exacting work.

miniature. It is the writer's guess, however, that while the furniture styles the craftsman chooses to copy may be one or two hundred years old, the toys he selects will be those he played with as a child.

Since most wood toys are painted in bright colors, there is no need to use valuable hardwood in their construction. Flat toys and playroom furniture can be sawed from scraps of plywood and softwood, while balsa is the ideal material for making shaped toys such as the rocking horse and the head of the stick horse shown in the illustration.

To shape the rocking horse, the under area was sawed first, the end triangles between the legs next, and the upper, outside line last. This produced the block horse shown in the illustration. The rest of the shaping was done by hand with sandpaper and files. If the craftsman feels that such shaping is hard to do, he is urged to try it. He will be surprised at how quickly the work will be finished.

The horse's tail and mane are of wool yarn, the saddle and reins of glove leather and the rockers, painted a bright orange, sawed from pine.

When it is time to make miniature toys, Polyform comes into

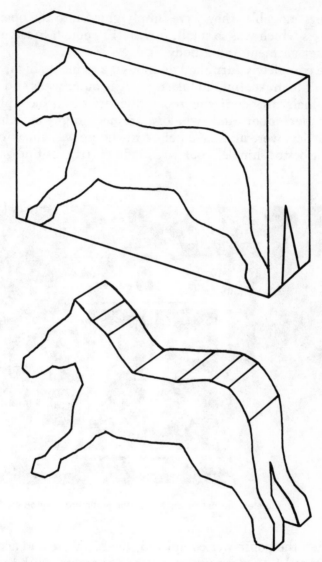

Rocking horse sawed from balsa wood can easily be sanded to shape.

its own. It was used for the circus animals, the mane of the stick
horse, the head and hands of the roly-poly, and the head and
limbs of the Raggedy Ann doll. In order to make the doll's arms

and legs movable, they were simply glued into the openings in the dress which was so small, it was stiff enough to serve as both an outer garment and a body.

The completely furnished dollhouse, 2 ⅛ inches high, was not difficult to make, but did take time. The outer walls and roof are of ¹⁄₁₆-inch plywood, the room dividers of ¹⁄₃₂-inch plywood. Wallpaper, door and window frames, rugs, curtains, and chandeliers were all added before the house was glued together. The "asbestos shingle" roof was made of strips of fine-grit sand-paper.

Completely furnished dollhouse for miniature playroom.

When the house was completed, the furniture and accessories were glued into place with the use of tweezers. With the exception of the brass bed, all the furniture is made of wood. Yet, if the reader would like to duplicate such a house, the tiny furniture could very well be made of cardboard or stiff paper. The house itself, however, should be made of wood.

Methods for constructing toys are no different from those used for any larger piece. The only advice to be offered the craftsman who hesitates to try his hand at making a few of these very small pieces is that if he does not, he will have missed a great deal of fun.

Flowers and House Plants

No respectable miniature home should be expected to do without a few bowls of flowers or a green plant or two. Plants and flowers denote the general period of a house only to a somewhat lesser degree than the furniture styles themselves.

Every miniature home needs plants and flowers.

A Victorian or early twentieth-century house would likely have on display flamboyant greenery in oversized containers— large-leaved philodendron or dieffenbachia, or gaudy fountains of cascading ferns. An elegant home of an earlier or later period might be more discreet and favor roses or other garden flowers in fine glass or silver containers. Middle-class homes of almost any period would have pots of begonias and geraniums on windowsills, and, always, ferns and other greenery.

The writer has certainly not thought of all the ways such plants and flowers can be made, but a few of them are described here, and the craftsman can devise others of his own.

Almost every large-leaved ornamental plant, and some rooted, flowering plants have visible stems. Because it can be bent to any desired shape, the thinnest copper or brass wire is ideal for making these stems. It should be cut to lengths a little longer than needed and painted a fairly dark green with an oil-base paint that will stick. In most cases, the wires should be bent to the approximate shapes wanted before leaves are added; too much handling afterwards might cause the leaves to drop off.

Ferns

To make a fern frond, a straight length of wire (which does not need to be painted, since it will not show) is glued to the center of a strip of crepe paper, as illustrated. A second strip is glued on top, encasing the wire. The paper should be pressed tightly against the wire and stretched a little as it is glued so that a ridge shows down the center. The paper is then cut into a long triangle with a soft point, as illustrated. If the paper is not the shade of green desired, it can be painted with watercolors. A few narrow, short fronds should be painted a lighter green at the tips. These can later be curled into leaves that have only partially opened and can be placed in the center of the arrangement.

Making a pot of ferns.

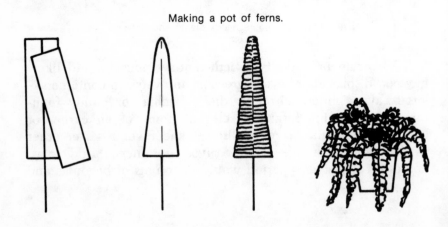

The edges of the frond are then fringed all the way to the center wire with sharp scissors and the wire curved as desired. The last step is to shorten the wire and arrange the frond, along with a generous number of others, in a container.

Ornamental Leaf Plants

Although almost any material (such as a sheet of plastic or colored paper) can be used for the leaves of ornamental plants, they will look more realistic if not perfectly flat. Cutting them from selected areas of small but full-sized plastic leaves will give them natural curves that will add greatly to their appearance. A single spray of plastic leaves, as small and thin as can be found, will furnish all the plants that could possibly be used in any miniature home.

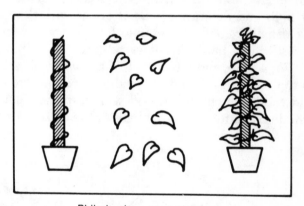

Philodendron on a standard.

The leaves should be cut in various shapes and sizes from different areas of the full-sized leaf so that some of them will curl rather deeply, some only slightly, and others not at all. Small slits are cut, as shown in the illustration, in the edge of each leaf where it will be attached to the stem.

Lengths of painted wire are then curved as desired and arranged in a container. If the plant is to be a vine, a long, single wire can be curled around a standard, as illustrated.

Each leaf is then fastened to the wire by placing a small dot of adhesive on the underside of the slit and pushing it onto the wire. Contact cement, while less convenient to handle than glue, will take hold immediately and the work will go faster. Duco can also be used if desired, but the leaf will then have to be held in place for a short while until the adhesive has partially dried. Although plants made in this way cannot stand rough handling, they are sturdy and, if carefully made, look very real.

Flowers

It is with some hesitancy that the writer mentions the word "Polyform" again, and promises that this will be the last time. It is, however, the ideal material for modeling tiny petals, leaves, and stems. The illustrations show a bowl of garden flowers in the making. Stems can be rolled between the palm and fingers, baked, then cut into needed lengths. Daisies are made by rolling five tiny balls and flattening them together with the fingers. A sixth, even smaller, ball can be used for a center. A long stem, covered with tiny balls, becomes a spray of delphinium or larkspur. For a rose, the lower half of a small, very thin oval is rolled in the fingers as shown. After the flower has been shaped, continued rolling of the lower end will form the stem. Leaves can be made by flattening small balls of the material and shaping them into triangles.

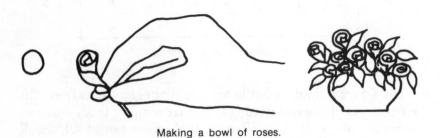

Making a bowl of roses.

Although flowers can be attached to baked stems and a second baking done, it is simpler to shape flowers and stems separately and bake them at the same time. Stems can then be attached to the flowers with Duco. Since moving pieces before baking might

BOWL OF GARDEN FLOWERS

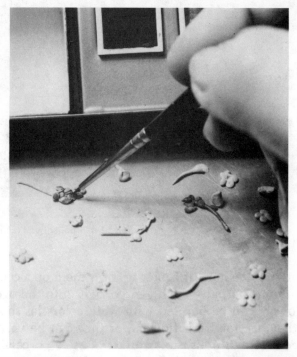

Shaped, baked flowers and stems are painted with watercolors.

Stems are glued to flowers, and arranging begins. Putty holds stems in place.

Completed arrangement is ¾ inch high. A coat of nail polish would turn it into a "porcelain" arrangement.

push them out of shape, it is best to form them on a cookie sheet or the bottom of a pan which can go right into the oven.

The flowers can be painted with watercolors, as shown, and used as they are for fresh flowers, or they can be varnished or given a coat of nail polish to simulate glass or porcelain.

Some very small natural flowers, seeds, and grasses can be dried and used in miniature arrangements. Baby's breath or a few individual flowerets of ageratum (or of any flower that grows in clusters and dries well) will make attractive bouquets for a miniature table. After drying, such flowers can be painted any color. The tips of grass blades, dried flat and painted green, can be used for the leaves of such flowers as irises and tulips.

These suggestions for miniature arrangements are only a sampling of the possibilities that await the craftsman. When making small flowers, the only important point to remember is strict adherence to the scale.

Mirrors
Although highly polished, chrome-plated or stainless-steel mirrors can be used on miniature furniture, there is no satisfactory substitute for glass mirrors. Unfortunately, silvering mirrors is

not a feasible home project and, while some mirror shops are willing to silver small pieces of shaped glass, the work requires special handling and the cost is relatively high.

Ready-made mirrors, such as those found in compacts, can be cut to desired shapes and sizes at home. If the miniature mirror will have straight sides, and if the edges will be concealed by a frame (and may therefore be left rough) the only tool needed is a diamond glass cutter. If the edges are to be rounded, or if there are to be tight angles, a diamond pencil and a pair of snub-nose pliers will be needed as well.

Miniature mirrors of any shape can be given beveled edges.

Polishing and beveling the edges is a more complicated process, and will require a 6- to 8-inch, 100-grit grinding wheel, powered at approximately 1000 rpm. Although a dry wheel will do the work, one with a water cup and spigot to keep the wheel wet is less likely to chip the glass edges. It is also more convenient to use a wheel that revolves in a horizontal, rather than a vertical, position. Ideal for the purpose is a small gem-cutting and grinding tool such as the one shown in the illustrations.

For best results, the mirror glass should be thin, preferably not over $\frac{1}{16}$ inch thick, and the protective coating of paint on the back should be in good condition. If the paint has begun to deteriorate and is loose in spots, it may flake off the edges when the glass is cut and spoil the new small mirror.

A paper pattern will be needed for cutting all mirrors, both straight-sided and curved. The shape wanted should first be drawn on graph paper, cut out along the drawn lines, and fastened with white glue to the back of the mirror.

Using a sharp knife, the outline of the pattern is then traced to cut through the mirror's backing to the glass. This will allow the diamond point of the cutter to reach the glass without scraping off parts of the backing from under the pattern.

The cutter is then used to scratch the glass along the pattern lines. Moderate pressure is used for this operation. If the pressure is too light, the depth of the scratch may not be uniform along its entire length; if too heavy, the glass may break. The glass should be supported on a perfectly smooth surface such as a thick, clean piece of wood.

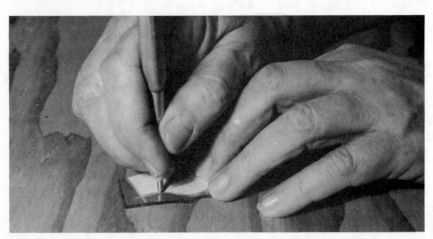

Scratching glass around pattern edge with diamond pencil.

Cutting a Straight-Sided Mirror

When cutting a straight-sided mirror, a ruler should be used as a guide for the cutter. If the mirror's edges are later to be smoothed by grinding, the scratch (the line made by the cutter on the glass) should be made about ⅟₆₄ inch outside the pattern edge. If no grinding is planned, the scratch should be made right at the pattern edge.

The excess material outside of the scratched lines is then broken off, one side at a time, by positioning the work in a large vise with wood faces, and allowing the part covered by the pattern to extend above the vise. The scratch along which the break is to be made should be exactly flush with the tops of the wood faces, and in front, facing the craftsman. The vise is then clamped just tight enough to hold the work firmly in position. Clamping too tightly could shatter the glass, but if the mirror is held too loosely, the planned break might not be a clean one.

If the glass is fairly wide, it is then broken off along the scratched line by holding a ruler (or any similar flat piece) so that it covers the exposed work surface, and snapping the glass straight backward. A narrow piece may be broken with the fingers, as illustrated.

Breaking straight edge of mirror along scratched line.

Cutting a Curved Edge

Any mirror with curves or angles that make the breaking-off process impossible to do will take more time to shape. The pattern is scratched with a diamond pencil, either at the edge or $\frac{1}{64}$ inch outside it, as previously explained. The pencil should be moved slowly and firmly to make a continuous, uniform scratch. Since the removal of excess glass outside the curved, scratched line is a fairly tedious process, the work will be made easier if as much of it as possible is first removed by the straight-line, snapping-off process explained above. This can be done by scratching as many straight lines as necessary, tangent to the curve, as shown in the illustration.

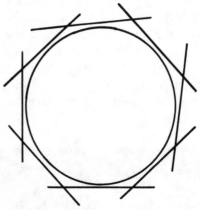

To shape round mirror, excess glass is first removed by straight-line, breaking-off process.

After removing as much excess glass as possible by the straight-line breaking method, the work is held in one hand, pattern-side up, and snub-nose pliers in the other hand are used to crush and nibble away the remaining excess glass in tiny pieces not much larger than coarse grains of sand. The nibbling away is done right up to the scratched line all around. If the edges are to be concealed by a frame, the mirror is now ready to use.

Grinding and Beveling Straight Edges

A straight edge is ground on the top side of a horizontal grinding wheel. The water cup spigot should be adjusted so there will be a generous flow of water on the wheel. Even if a glass is to be beveled, the edges should first be ground until they are smooth, square and even with the edges of the paper pattern.

The glass should be held squarely and firmly against the wheel at a 90-degree angle to the diameter of the wheel. This will allow the wheel to scrape the glass edge nearly lengthwise. Care should be taken not to tilt the glass to either side and not to press down harder on one end than the other. Progress should be checked frequently. If one end is grinding down faster than the other, the glass should be repositioned by switching ends. This should be done as often as necessary to keep the grinding uniform along the entire edge.

If a dry grinding wheel is used, pressure should be very light. Frequent pauses during the work will help to prevent the glass from becoming overheated, which could result in breakage.

When the glass has been ground to the edges of the paper pattern, the mirror may be used as it is, or the edges may be beveled.

To bevel a straight edge, the glass is held at an angle against the wheel top, using the same method described above. Although a bevel may be cut at any angle, the glass is more easily held steady if the angle is not more than 45 degrees. If the bevels are to meet at the corners, all edges must be beveled to the same depth and at the same angle.

Grinding and Beveling Convex Curves
Convex curves, such as those on round or oval mirrors, are also ground on the top of the horizontal grinding wheel. The process

Grinding edge of round mirror.

is the same as that used for grinding a straight edge, except the glass must be rotated continually. The easiest method is to grind a short arc at a time by rocking the glass edge back and forth on the wheel, then continuing in a series of overlapping arcs until the edge is smooth and flat.

Beveling a convex edge is done in the same way, with the glass being held at the desired angle. Great care must be taken to keep the bevel angle uniform throughout, and frequent inspections of the progress should be made.

Grinding and Beveling Concave Curves and Angles

Grinding concave (inside) curves is a much more difficult process. These must be ground on the edge or "corner" of the wheel where the top meets the side. If the wheel is new, this edge has a sharp, right angle that will bite into the glass very quickly. Although, with care, a new wheel may be used, it is better to round off the edge with a wheel dresser and to turn the wheel over in the grinder when a sharp edge is needed for other jobs.

When grinding a concave curve, the glass must be held so that the grinding action is crosswise to the glass edge, as illustrated. Since this increases the possibility of chipping the edge, the pressure of the glass against the wheel must be extremely light, and the glass must be kept in constant motion up and down across the wheel edge to keep the wheel from digging in at any one spot.

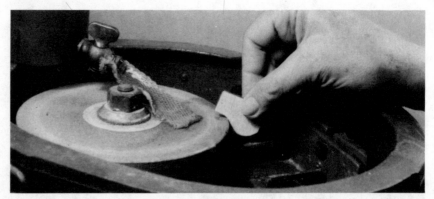

Grinding concave edge on corner of wheel.

To grind an inside angle, the side of the wheel with the sharp edge should be used. It is only necessary to hold the edges of the angle against the wheel's top and side and grind both edges at once. To bevel an inside angle, the glass is held in the same position as above. However, since tilting the glass makes it impossible for both edges to touch the wheel at once, each edge must be beveled separately.

When all cutting and grinding has been done, the paper pattern on the back of the mirror may be soaked in water and rubbed off. There is some danger, however, that the mirror's backing may be damaged in the process. Since the paper will not show, and will furnish a good surface for glueing the mirror to the furniture, it is safer to leave it on.

12

Making a Player Piano

The procedure followed for making the player piano shown here is illustrated in the following pages. This particular piece was chosen for this chapter because—with the exception of the carved panels which are optional—the entire piece can be made with just one power tool—a jigsaw. If the carved sections are to be included, an electric hand drill will also be needed. The piano is three inches high.

As a first step, front and side views are drawn on graph paper as shown. In this case, patterns for all the pieces to be cut have been drawn at one time, but this is not usually advisable. It is better to draw and cut parts for one section (such as all the pieces below the keyboard), glue those to the foundation, then draw and cut pieces for the center section and so on. In this way the pattern can be adjusted from time to time as necessary.

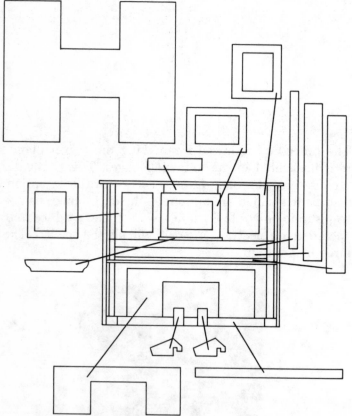

Front view of player piano with patterns for parts.

Although rosewood is used for this piano, any other hardwood will do as well. The H-shaped foundation piece is also made of rosewood. This is an extravagance since only the areas around

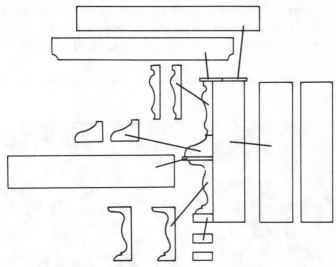

Side view of player piano with patterns for parts.

the carvings and a narrow margin around the base will show. The foundation can very well be cut from softwood, in which case extra care will have to be given in finishing the exposed areas because of the difference in color and grain of the two woods.

1. The foundation piece is sawed first so that other pieces can be checked against it as they are cut.

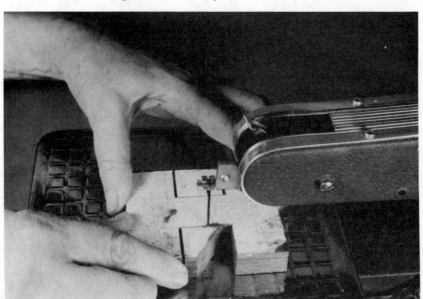

1.

2.   Patterns for the rest of the pieces to be sawed are next glued to slices of wood of selected thicknesses. Although these thicknesses are approximately correct, there will be enough difference between some of them and the original drawing to make a few necessary adjustments in the pattern as the work goes along.

2.

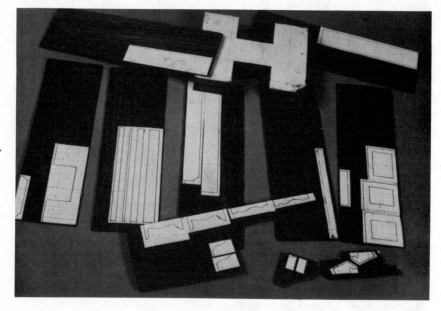

3.   One leg of the foundation piece has been sawed off to permit access to the opposing inner faces. A hole for one end of the wire that will support the music roller is then drilled with a pin vise. (It would be almost impossible to drill these holes accurately from the outside inward.) Because the leg will later be glued back into place, and because the joint will not show, the cut has been made roughly so that glueing it back in exactly the same place can more easily be done.

Also shown are the three frames to be sawed, and holes which have been made in preparation for inside cuts. The thin brass wire will be inserted through the roller.

4.   A matching hole is drilled in the other leg of the founda-

3.

4.

tion piece. The roller has been sanded to shape from a small block of balsa wood, and the wire pushed through it.

5.

6.

5.   The ends of the brass wire, holding the roller, have been inserted into the drilled holes and the leg glued into place. A

cover for the back of the piano has been cut from $\frac{1}{32}$-inch plywood, and a piece to fill the opening at the bottom from $\frac{1}{16}$-inch plywood.

6.   Since the inner faces of the foundation piece would be difficult to reach later on, they are given a coat of walnut stain at this point. They will hardly be seen, so additional finishing will not be needed.

7.

7.   All small pieces and those with curved edges have already been sawed. Only straight cuts are now left to do. The narrow blade is replaced with a wider one. Although this step is not necessary, the wide blade will help to make the cut edges straighter so that less filing will be needed later.

8.   With all the pieces cut, the paper patterns have been removed and the rubber cement rubbed off the wood. The work of sanding surfaces and filing edges now begins.

9.   Supports for the pedals are prepared next. They will be hooked over the wood rail as shown, and the pedals glued to them. These pot metal pedals were found in a model boat kit

8.

9.

and have been painted black. Since not every craftsman is apt to make such a lucky find, the pedals can be made of wood, preferably ridged with a narrow file, or of black corduroy glued to pieces of $\frac{1}{32}$-inch plywood.

The $\frac{1}{16}$-inch plywood section has been glued into place between the lower legs of the foundation piece.

10. Glueing the supports to the rail will hold them firmly in place. For the sake of appearance, however, heads and short sections of two brass pins will be inserted into drilled holes to give the impression that the supports are held in place by a brass shaft. The pedals will not be glued on until the assembled supports have been fastened to the piano.

10.

11. Thin pieces of wood to be carved have been sawed to shape and a tentative design drawn. The wood pieces have been fastened with rubber cement to plywood, so that they can more easily be carved. Since the carvings should be similar, matching lines will be cut on each panel in turn.

12. The "music" is drawn on a strip of paper with a fine pen and india ink. The strip will then be glued around the roller.

13. The work of filling the sanded wood begins. The filler

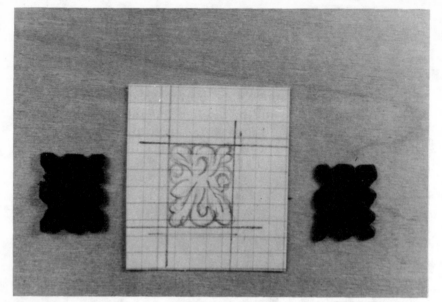

11.

12.

has been colored walnut. Part of the area that will not show is being left unfilled in order to leave some raw wood for later glueing.

13.

14. Glueing is begun. Only the back, side facings, bottom railing, feet, and the lower facing (shown being glued) will be fastened to the foundation at this point. Because all the pieces of

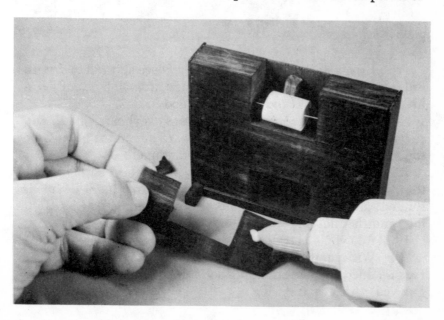

14.

this piano have good, flat glueing surfaces, white glue will be the only adhesive used.

15.   Before further glueing is done, areas that will be exposed are given a coat of walnut stain. The rest of the pieces will be filled and stained separately before they are glued into place.

15.

16.   Excess stain is wiped off and the piece allowed to dry. In order to hold the roller in a fixed position, a small block of wood has been glued to it, and to the plywood back.

17.   Glueing is continued. The legs, keyboard shelf, and curved pieces at each end of the keyboard are added next. Glue squeeze-out is being removed with a toothpick.

18.   The center section, consisting of the keyboard lid, the thin board beneath it, and the molding behind it will be filled, stained, and added next. The lid has been rounded off by sanding, and the molding shaped with a round file.

19.   A keyhole is drilled in the lid with a pin vise.

20.   With most of the parts now glued into place, the music rack is added. Like the molding behind the keyboard, it has been grooved with a round file.

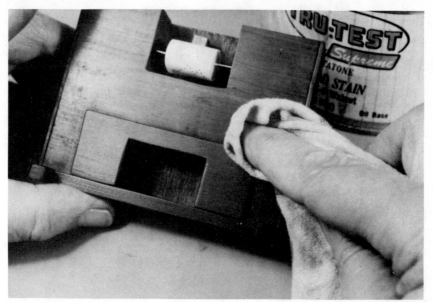

16.

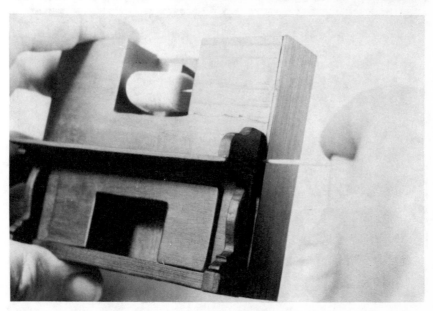

17.

21.   Before the center frame is added, a strip to bridge the gap between the upper legs of the foundation piece is glued into place.

18.

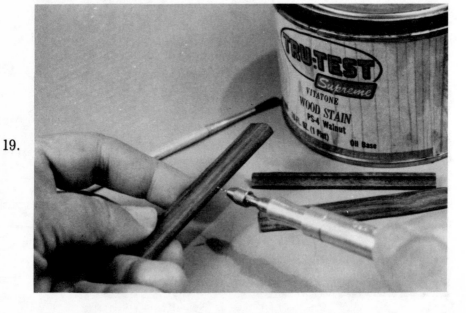

19.

22. The two halves of the top are added next.
23. Joints between the two curved side pieces are con-

20.

21.

spicuous. A dab of wood filler in each will solve the problem. A single link of a thin chain has been glued over the keyhole.

22.

23.

24. The piano has been waxed and polished. Four pieces of wood, about the size of tiny beads, have been glued at the cor-

24.

ners on the bottom to lift the piano just a fraction of an inch off the floor. As a final step, "hinges" are glued into the cracks on the center top and at the back of the keyboard lid. These consist of lengths of very thin brass wire which is sold in hobby and model train supply shops. If thin enough wire cannot be found, it would be better to omit this step altogether.

Index

225